JOURNOLISTS

JOHN KOSKI is Associate Editor of *YOU* Magazine. His life is a constant struggle against listlessness. Together with Mitchell Symons he is also the author of *Movielists*.

MITCHELL SYMONS is a former BBC TV director who writes for a variety of publications, including a regular column in the *Sunday Times*. As well as writing lists, he devises television game shows and compiles fiendishly difficult crosswords.

JOURNOLISTS

1992

John Koski and Mitchell Symons

Cartoons by Ian Dicks

CHAPMANS

Chapmans Publishers Ltd
141–143 Drury Lane
London WC2B 5TB

First published by Chapmans 1992

A CIP catalogue record for this book
is available from the British Library

ISBN 1–85592–733–0

Photoset in Linotron Times by
MC Typeset Ltd, Wouldham, Rochester, Kent

Printed and bound in Great Britain by
Clays Ltd, St Ives plc

ACKNOWLEDGEMENTS

The fight against listlessness continues!
Welcome to the fourth *YOU* Magazine
book of *Journolists*. Once again we must
thank Sara Driver and Patricia Martin for
their invaluable research and the following
contributors for their invaluable lists:
Malcolm Burgess, Donnie Kerr, Steve
Clothier, John Machin and Clive
Whichelow.

CONTENTS

The Way We Live Now   9

Films   33

Sport   38

Quotations   45

Music   53

Literature and the Media   62

For the Record   68

Miscellany   80

Ten rules which should be in the Citizen's Charter

Anyone using the last of the toilet paper must immediately inform the other occupants of the building

All employed people will have the right to phone in sick at least once during Wimbledon fortnight

Parents who name their children after the entire local football team will be obliged to undergo counselling

Any television programme of a broadly Australian nature must be preceded by a public warning

Shoppers seeing evidence of Christmas promotions before 1 August will be entitled to a free £10 gift voucher

Employees who are shouted at by their boss will have the right to remove the air from his or her tyres

Customers invited to 'Have a nice day' will be entitled to empty the contents of a can of Coke over the well-wisher's head

Viewers who spot Anneka Rice, Terry Wogan or Noel Edmonds on more than three separate occasions in one week can claim a licence refund

People at the head of any queue will be addressed as 'Sir' or 'Madam' by all those behind them

Anyone driving at 20mph on a public highway while wearing a flat cap and smoking a pipe will have his licence taken away

Unlicensed jester – demand a refund

Are you a workaholic? Ten tell-tale signs

You make Christmas dinner a working lunch
You've accumulated so much holiday, you should have retired two years ago
You're the only sober passenger on the last train home
The last Saturday you had off was to watch England win the soccer World Cup
You've got a phone extension in the garden
You haven't noticed that your children left home several years ago
Your last foreign holiday was a school exchange trip
The paper you buy on the way home is tomorrow's
You don't recognise the people in the family photo on your desk
Your best friends are the office cleaners

Modern manners – ten posers for the 1990s

Is it permissible to hold a conversation during a TV dinner?
Do you raise your little finger while drinking a pint of lager top?
Is it polite to talk to an answerphone with your mouth full?
Is it rude to point at an identity parade?
How do you open an automatic door for a lady?
Is it acceptable to offer your bus seat to a pregnant feminist?
Should you remove your baseball cap when a funeral cortège passes by?
Is it polite to leave the street corner while somebody else is still eating their Big Mac?
Should you send a 'Thank you' letter after an acid house party?
Can you take your own sandwiches to a royal garden party?

Ten entries from the Businessman's Book of Quotes

A man who is tired of lunch is tired of life
There are lies, damned lies and expense accounts
A week is a long time in office politics
To lose one account may be regarded as a misfortune; to lose two looks like carelessness
There is no such thing as a free luncheon voucher
From each according to his abilities, to each according to his abilities
Never in the field of investment borrowing has so much been owed by so many to so few
I have nothing to declare except my dividend
Better working late than never
Give us the cheque and we'll finish the job

Captain Bob, expensively accounted for – quote

Are you an anorak? Ten warning signs

Your glasses are held together with Sellotape

You can reel off all the names in the Monty Python cheese-shop sketch

You never leave home without a plastic carrier bag

You have a stain on your anorak where your ballpoint has leaked

You have *Bradshaw's Railway Guide* out on extended loan from the library

You can find Radio 5

You spend excessive amounts of time alone in your bedroom with the door shut

You wear purple nylon Y-fronts

You're working on a scale model of the Channel Tunnel

You have a cream shirt with a spoon collar

Ten really useful functions for neighbourhood watch schemes

To keep an eye out for water company officials during a hosepipe ban

To find out who keeps pinching your parking space

To warn you when door-to-door salesmen are in the area

To find out who slurs *My Way* at 11.30 every Friday night

To push free newspapers through your letterbox when you're on holiday

To log sightings of road sweepers

To find out who throws empty chip packets in your front garden

To stop and search young men with short hair carrying bibles

To make a note of who takes stuff from builders' skips

To pick off carol singers

Pub grub – a guide to interpretation

'Traditional menu': *Chips with everything*

'Vegetarian special': *Salad*

'Tasty jacket potato': *We've got a microwave!*

'Garnish': *Single, limp lettuce leaf (re-usable)*

'Chilli con carne': *Shepherd's pie without the potato topping*

'Today's special': *Yesterday's leftovers*

'Ploughman's lunch': *Bank clerk's lunch*

'Gâteau': *Sponge cake with a hefty price tag*

'Soup of the day': *Soup of the week*

'Cooked to your requirements': *Over-cooked to our specifications*

We're all executives now – ten updated job descriptions

'Surplus domestic commodities analyst': *Rag-and-bone man*

'Liquid protein manager': *Tea lady*

'Mobile cash-flow accumulator': *Beggar*

'Multi-level personnel re-locator': *Lift operator*

'Scholastic urban controller': *Lollipop lady*

'Component re-cycling officer': *Dustman*

'Visual interface hygiene technician': *Window cleaner*

'Speculative investment consultant': *Bookie*

'Mobile urban environmental specialist': *Road sweeper*

'Short-break travel and information adviser': *Taxi driver*

Keith, from street cred to sacred

Clive –
please give
generously

A plain man's guide to the New Age

Aromatherapy: *'Mmm, roast beef!'*
Dowsing: *Eight pints of Tetley's*
Sun-worshipping: *Drooling over Page Three*
Positive vibrations: *Living under the
Heathrow flight path*
Chanting: *'Here we go, here
we go, here we go . . .'*
Astral projection: *Bonfire night*
Numerology: *'One-hundred and eighty!'*
Aura reading: *The latest Stephen King novel*
Sacred Stones: *Mick and Keith*
Ley lines: *Essex girls queueing for a disco*

Ten new charities

Help the Waged: *No more carping about company
chairmen's salary increases*
Save the Wales: *Keeping Charles and Di together*
Doxfam: *Making time for junior hospital doctors to
have meals*
Dancer Research: *Whatever happened to the
lambada?*
International Read Dross: *Keep pulp fiction out of
airport lounges*
National Truss: *Caring support for royal polo
injuries*
Clive Aid: *Help Clive James to get a decent TV
show*
British Harp Foundation: *Grants for lager louts*
Help the Hopeless: *Let's find a decent Eurovision
song for Norway*
RSPCA: *Royal Society for the Prevention of Coffee
Adverts*

Kapow, blam, stickemup – big bucks in any language

Third World-speak – a guide to interpretation

'Developing': *Under-developed*
'Under-developed': *Only one TV channel*
'Cultural imperialism': *Starsky and Hutch dubbed into the local dialect*
'Aid': *Our government gives money to buy British goods*
'Loans': *Our banks give money and then write it off*
'Popular revolution': *Popular with the people who've seized power*
'Free elections': *Results freely available before the votes have been cast*
'Emergency relief': *Here comes another pop concert*
'National father figure': *Old dictator*
'Local customs': *Corruption*

Timeshare-speak – a guide to interpretation

'Congratulations, you have been chosen . . . ': *Along with the rest of the country*
'You have won a car, a yacht or an alarm clock': *Just guess which one you'll get*
'Enjoy free holidays for the rest of your life': *Apart from the four-figure service charges*
'Have you considered a holiday investment?': *Don't mention the word 'timeshare'*
'Attend our presentation and have a drink on us': *It could be the most expensive glass of wine you ever have*
'Exciting holiday development': *As yet unbuilt*
'Absolutely no commitment to buy': *This only applies to investigative journalists*
'Low season bargains': *Two weeks of biting wind and freezing rain in a Scottish pine forest*
'Exclusive location': *Spain*
'You can exchange your two weeks for holidays in resorts around the world': *Florida*

Is your neighbourhood in decline? Ten tell-tale signs

Someone steals the Neighbourhood Watch sign
Your street is used for a jeans advert
The pit bulls go round in pairs
A religious cult buys the house on the corner
Squatters begin to move out voluntarily
The postman walks round in full riot gear
Every house has a satellite dish
The window cleaner offers a boarding-up service
It is impossible to clamp cars as they have no wheels
The government gives a grant to hold a garden festival

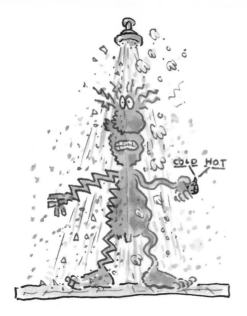

The world's ten smallest measurable quantities

The space on a motor insurance claim form for the crash diagram

The area described by estate agents as the 'fourth bedroom'

The amount of butter on a motorway cafeteria scone

The distance between passengers on a charter flight

The change from a £20 note in a London pub

The time between a boardroom vote of confidence and a soccer manager being sacked

The movement between ice-cold and super-heated steam on a shower control knob

The legroom in the back of a Renault 5

The number of laughs in a British sitcom

The size of the small print on privatisation commercials

Planning next year's holiday? A consumers' guide

'Touring holiday': *Spend all day looking for somewhere to spend the night*

'Self-catering holiday': *Bacon-and-egg breakfasts abroad*

'Cruising holiday': *Nowhere to run, nowhere to hide*

'Full-board holiday': *Two weeks of inedible dinners*

'Boating holiday': *Rivers of tears*

'Coach holiday': *If it's Tuesday, we've still got five days to go*

'Holiday centre holiday': *Holiday camp holiday*

'Activity holiday': *Learn to scuba-dive in the hotel swimming pool*

'Package holiday': *Make yourself sick at the taverna barbecue*

'Camping holiday': *Don't forget to pack the toilet paper*

Ten names for inner-city pubs

The Tattooed Arms
The King's Head-Butt
The Duck and Dive
The Spreadeagled
The Brickthrower's Arms
The Old Brawl and Bush
The Rose and Crowned
The Police Horse and Groom
The Ram and Flag
The Strip and Search

Builder-speak – a guide to interpretation

'You called me just in time': *I was about to go out of business*

'You wouldn't believe the price of materials': *You won't believe what I'm going to charge you*

'Have you thought about green?': *I've got five drums of green paint left over from my last job*

'I need to pop back to the yard for some tools': *I'm off to the pub*

'We can start right away': *We'll turn your place into a bomb site and then go off and start another job*

'You should never mess with electrics': *That'll be £20 to change a fuse*

'This whole wall will have to be redone': *There's a tiny damp patch in one corner*

'You'll hardly notice we're here': *We hardly ever will be here*

'I'll have to charge you for extras': *Like turning up*

'We should be finished by October': *But I can't guarantee which year*

Home help – ten questions which house surveys should address

How many layers of wallpaper there are in the living room

If the Salvation Army band marches past on Sunday mornings

Whether you need a 50-foot aerial mast to get decent TV reception

If the phone number is almost identical with that of the local minicab firm

Whether the hideous polystyrene ceiling tiles are fixed with Superglue

How often charity collectors call

If there's a reliable window cleaner locally

The real reason why the owner is selling

If the children next door are learning a musical instrument

Whether the central heating rattles in the middle of the night

Ten tell-tale signs of a privatised NHS

Patients will be called customers

Staff will say things like: 'Hi, I'm Bob and I'm your surgeon for today'

You will be wheeled in to the Beazer Homes Casualty Unit

Hospitals will offer 'frequent user' discounts

Ambulances will have first- and second-class compartments

The medication trolley will have Access and Visa stickers on it

Fundraising ambulance-boot sales will be held on Sunday mornings

Prescription forms will have ads on the back of them

Nurses will administer injections with a cheery 'Have a nice day!'

Hospitals will publish league tables of mortality rates

Not a des res, even with a band

The ten laws of gardening

Nothing ever looks like it does on the seed packet

Your lawn is always slightly bigger than your desire to mow it

Whichever garden tool you want is always at the back of the shed

The only way to ensure rain is to give the garden a good soaking

Weeds grow at precisely twice the rate you can pull them out

Autumn follows summer, winter follows autumn, frost follows planting

Evergreens go a funny shade of brown in the winter

The only way to guarantee some colour all year round is to buy a gnome

However bare the lawn, grass will appear in the cracks between the patio paving stones

'Annuals' mean disappointment once a year

'A man who is tired of London is tired of . . .'

Hustlers trying to wash your windscreen at traffic lights

Unintelligible public announcements on the Underground

Being asked directions to 'Lychester Square'

The letterbox clogged with cards from minicab firms

Having to park three streets from your house

Not being able to afford any of the things which attract tourists

Northerners complaining what a struggle life is

Driving for an hour to have dinner at a friend's house

Politically correct councils

Down-and-outs with 'I'm hungry' signs around their necks

Do you need assertiveness training? Ten tell-tale signs

You pull in to let milk floats overtake

All three political parties have you down as a certainty

You always say 'yes' when shop assistants ask if you need any help

You're never 'too busy' to answer an opinion poll

Geese say 'Boo!' to you

You give up your seat on the bus to schoolchildren

You never tell a taxi driver he's going the wrong way

The cupboard under the sink is stuffed with dusters bought on the doorstep

You're struggling to keep up the payments on all the insurance policies you've got

You never correct people when they get your name wrong

Paranoia! Ten things guaranteed to make you feel guilty

Going through customs

Overtaking a police car

Phoning in sick

Watching TV when you're off sick

Walking out of a shop which has security guards at the door

Leaving a supermarket without buying anything

Going to church once a year for the Christmas carol service

Sitting in a cinema on your own

Not leaving a tip at a restaurant

Going through an unmanned ticket barrier

Keep taking the pils – ten reasons not to give up drinking

You'd feel like a party pooper at communion

You've just bought a *Good Beer Guide*

How else could you justify a three-hour business lunch?

Imagine karaoke nights sober

What else are you going to smuggle through customs?

A stiff Perrier after work just isn't the same

How would you get through Friday nights at the local Indian?

It could destroy your chances of being a champion darts player

It's the only way to survive the speeches at wedding receptions

The only exercise you get is walking down to the bottle bank

An Okey Kokey Karry Oke, a pils and a Hail Mary, please

The family that plays together . . . ten new nuggets of family lore

The family that smokes together chokes together

The family that dines together whines together

The family that drinks together sinks together

The family that shops together drops together

The family that works together shirks together

The family that views together snoozes together

The family that weeds together bleeds together

The family that eats together bleats together

The family that hikes together wears Nikes together

The family that sails together wails together

A ten-point parents' charter

Parents should not be required to do handstands under any circumstances

Christmas begins in mid-December – it is nothing whatsoever to do with summer or autumn

Parents must be allowed access to the phone, perhaps once an evening

Meals out do not invariably have to be at Pizzaland – occasionally make it Pizza Hut

Parity with what the kids next door get is not an acceptable basis for pocket money negotiations

Parents cannot be expected to answer questions like 'What is the sky?' at three o'clock in the morning (or at any time, for that matter)

They require rest and recuperation centres (known as bedrooms)

All shops selling batteries will be open on Christmas Day

Pets bought to teach children the concept of death will duly oblige

Parents should be allowed to win the occasional Nintendo game

Funny Valentines – a guide to the personal columns on 14 February

'Fluffy bunny-wunny': *Sex maniac with a body hair problem*

'Hunky love commando': *Branch librarian*

'Dimples': *Oversized lady with a tendency to remove her false teeth after five port and lemons*

'Biggles': *Moped rider with own leather gloves*

'Mr Toad': *Man with a serious wart condition*

'Pussykins': *Sheds hair all over the place*

'Mr Whippy': *Retired judge*

'Snow queen': *Girl with a serious dandruff problem*

'Big boy': *Shelf-stacker at the local supermarket*

'Bow-wow': *Barking mad*

Are you pretentious?
Ten tell-tale signs

Your children go to orchestra conducting lessons

You ask for 'Two Cornetti'

You're shopping around for a mock-Tudor satellite dish

You demand first-class tickets on the miniature railway

Your cat is on BUPA

Your address is embossed on your Post-it notes

You boast of having read *Maigret* in the original French

You dress for the cinema

You wear monogrammed shell suits

You taste the lager in Indian restaurants before asking the waiter to pour it

Are you a post-New Man?
Ten tell-tale signs

You can whistle with a pipe clenched between your teeth

You put pepper on vindaloo curries

You can out-stare a rottweiler

You're a self-taught helicopter pilot

You've got leather elbow patches on your tweed jacket – but nobody thinks you're a polytechnic lecturer

The waiters don't sneer when you order your steak well done

You drive a sports car with the roof down in winter

You consider Oliver Reed to be a social drinker

You can grow a beard over the weekend

The only birth at which you were present was your own

John, the hunky love commando – just for a day

A single European currency – what it means to the *homme dans la rue*

We'll all get nostalgic for the miserable 5p piece

Bank notes will have pictures of Abba and Demis Roussos on them

You won't have to buy endless cups of coffee at foreign airports to use up holiday change

The Samaritans will be inundated with calls from coin collectors

The problem of Scottish £5 notes will disappear

We'll all spend two years saying 'What's that in old money?'

The number of Italian millionaires will be slashed overnight

Redundant 'Cambio/Change/Wechsel' staff will find work converting slot machines

Street traders won't be able to fiddle you on holiday

Banks will charge double commission to convert European money into other currencies

Order, order! A guide to parliamentary debates

'Can the Prime Minister confirm . . . ?': *Of course he can, since he gave me the question to ask in the first place*

'Is the Honourable Member aware . . . ?': *If he is, my researcher is fired*

'Most right-thinking people': *Me*

'The vast majority of the population': *My next-door neighbour*

'All working mothers': *My next-door neighbour's wife*

'I think the Honourable Member is misinformed': *He's lying*

'Our record speaks for itself': *I certainly can't think of anything to say for it*

'Our policy on this is absolutely clear': *We change it whenever it becomes unpopular*

'Will the Minister answer the question?': *And change the habit of a lifetime*

'Order, order!': *Thank God they haven't got any bread rolls to throw*

Ten sounds to strike terror into the heart of twentieth-century man

The death rattle of a washing machine not covered by extended warranty

The pub pianist's intro to *My Way*

The constant drip behind the false wall after the shower is turned off

The boss's 'So how long have you been with us?'

The first toy commercial of the festive season

The background noises when phoning home to see how the kids are managing on their own for the weekend

The pilot's 'There is no cause for alarm' announcement

The garage mechanic's ominous intake of breath

His name clearly enunciated in an otherwise unintelligible public announcement at a football match

The opening bars of next-door's Guns 'n' Roses double album

Don't lose your credibility – ten places you wouldn't want to be seen

Queueing for Chippendales' tickets

On a Benetton poster

In the easy listening section of a record shop

Behind Esther Rantzen on *That's Life!*

Opening a supermarket

At the complaints counter of a sex shop

On the front page of *Sunday Sport*

In the studio audience of *Kilroy*

At a Barbara Cartland book signing

Window shopping at Ratner's

So you've got an ology – just what does it mean?

Psychology: *You don't think of Freud as the presenter of* The Media Show

Ecology: *You know the location of all the bottle banks in your area*

Philology: *You know the meaning of the word 'philology'*

Biology: *You know your way around the back of the bike sheds*

Ornithology: *You can spot a Bill Oddie at fifty yards*

Meteorology: *You don't need to convert centigrade into fahrenheit*

Anthropology: *You've seen* Planet of the Apes *three times*

Geology: *You've got a collection of pebbles from the beach in your fruit bowl*

Graphology: *You always use a typewriter*

Sociology: *You can rationalise family arguments*

Know your road signs – a motorists' guide

'Motorway Ends': *Slow down to 70mph*

'Motorway Ahead': *D'ya feel lucky, punk?*

'Traffic Lights': *Beware windscreen cleaners*

'Roundabout': *Who dares wins*

'Dual Carriageway Ahead': *First chance for ten miles to overtake that bloody caravan*

'Dual Carriageway Ends': *Long tailback begins*

'Roadworks': *Two miles of traffic cones and not a workman in sight*

'No Services on Motorway': *It's a bit late to tell us now*

'Residents' Parking Only': *Non-residents double-parking*

'Mud on Road': *Tractor on road doing 3mph*

It's their first baby. Ten tell-tale signs

What was the box room is now 'the nursery'

They've acquired a whole new shelf of books

Nappy-changing is still an enjoyable novelty

They've asked the neighbours to stop smoking

They've taken three rolls of film of everything the baby's ever done – and it's only three days old

They rush to a medical book every time the baby coughs

The name Spock doesn't remind them of *Star Trek*

They all go to bed at the same time

He stops calling her 'Darling' and starts calling her 'Mummy'

They talk about programmes they've heard on the World Service

Are you politically correct? Ten tell-tale signs

You insist on your chips being wrapped in the *Guardian*

You told the opinion pollster you'd be voting Labour and did

You think *Little Women* is not only sexist, but sizeist too

You consider Essex girls an oppressed minority

You find flags in sandcastles imperialistic

You can't decide if strippers are exploited or boldly asserting a woman's right to choose

Your cat is vegetarian

Zebra crossings remind you of apartheid

When your children play cowboys and Indians, the 'American aboriginals' have to win

You think *Mastermind* is elitist

Spock – being a Vulcan is child's play

Teacher assessment – a guide to interpretation

'Has a comprehensive knowledge of the subject':
A right clever dick

'Communicates well with the students': *Has a prominent forefinger*

'Able to motivate colleagues': *Done time for GBH*

'Well liked by pupils': *Offers them cigarettes*

'Quietly serves the cause of education': *Constantly hungover*

'Able to resolve disputes quickly': *Deadly accurate with a board rubber*

'Gets involved in extra-curricular activities': *Goes drinking with the Upper Sixth*

'Has mastered the National Curriculum': *Unfortunately, the pupils haven't*

'Completely loyal': *Working for the pension*

'Creates an informal atmosphere': *Rioting in class*

Ten election-winning promises (Labour, take note)

Lower-income taxis

The repeal of Sod's Law

Quota reduction on soap imports (*Neighbours, Home and Away*, etc.)

Regeneration of the cities (Coventry City, Bristol City, York City, etc.)

Strict currency controls, i.e. no more coins like the 5p piece

Defence spending cuts (no more £2.5m central defenders)

Reducing inflation (of politicians' egos)

Compulsory testing of all seventy-year-old MPs

A ban on party-political broadcasts

Muzzling of chat-show hosts

Ten DIY products we're waiting for

Disposable paint brushes

Zero-gravity ceiling paper

Luminous fuses

Self-assembly furniture that actually does assemble itself

Suede-handled screwdrivers

Battery-operated wall lights

Clip-on bath taps

Shrink-to-fit kitchen tiles

A drill attachment that makes the coffee

Velcro wallpaper

Chunnel vision – ten excuses for delays

Fish on the line
Wrong sort of fish on the line
Leaky roof
Train went through the red channel at customs
Driver afraid of the dark
It's not late, it's the time difference
French farmers on the line
Ticket inspector suffering from rabies
Someone used the bidet while the train was stationary
Staff of life shortages (no *baguettes* in the buffet car)

Farming today – those rural terms explained

'Smallholding': *Size isn't everything*
'Set aside': *Something that provides for old age*
'Traditional ways': *Battery farming*
'Battery farming': *A farmer's right to choose*
'Free-range': *Bits of straw in the egg box*
'Organic produce': *Expensive*
'Gentleman farmer': *Former rock star*
'Crop rotation': *Wheat, barley, oats, golf course*
'Farm shop': *Shelves of designer mustards and brown bread ice-cream*
'Right of way': *Just try to find it*

Ten Nintendo games we're waiting for

Multi-Storey Car Parking
Find Radio 3!
Package Flight Seating Plan
Central London Driving Test
Super Maxwell Brothers
Motorway Toilet Search
The Sunday Trading Laws Maze
Shopping Trolley Challenge
Find Cher's Clothes
Quest for the British Rail Refund

Road test-speak – a guide to interpretation

'Impressive performance': *I didn't know I was breaking the speed limit, officer*
'Nippy': *Small with no chance of breaking the speed limit*
'Computer-designed': *Looks like every other car*
'Has all the extras': *Electric windows*
'Great fun': *Sports car that shakes your spine to jelly*
'Surprisingly generous boot space': *Provided you want to fill it with ping-pong balls and not suitcases*
'Practical': *Four doors*
'Economical': *You'll never use enough petrol to get the full set of lead crystal glasses*
'Sluggish': *Dangerous to overtake milk-floats*
'Top of the range': *Standard model with wire wheels*

Southern discomfort – ten signs of recession south of Watford Gap

Norman Tebbit tells you to 'Get in your Volvo'
Alan Bleasdale writes a play about your life
Wine bars advertise 'Unhappy Hours'
Visiting northern soccer fans wave wads of £10
    notes at you
The home fax machine is covered in cobwebs
Your diary has more windows than the
    greenhouses at Kew Gardens
Your only chance to power dress is when you go to
    the supermarket
Protest badges appear saying 'Sole Not Dole'
Auf Wiedersehen Pet is remade as a series
    following the exploits of a group of sacked
    German *au pairs*
The kids' Wendy houses are repossessed

Monday, Monday – ten good things about going back to work

No more DIY for five days
Free personal phone calls from the office
The kids out of the house by 8 am
No backseat drivers until Sunday
Calling the speaking clock whenever the boss
    hoves into view
The photocopier breaking down by 9.30 am
Getting paid to go to lunch
No difficult decisions, like whether to watch
    Lovejoy or *The Darling Buds of May*
The visiting relatives will have gone home
A bit of peace and quiet on the bus to work

Ten consequences of an independent Scotland

Membership of OPEC (Organisation of Plaid
    Exporting Countries)
Border guards patrolling Hadrian's Wall
Donald Where's Your Troosers in the Eurovision
    Song Contest
An economy built entirely on shortbread and dolls
    in national costume
Passport control officers on London to Edinburgh
    trains
Membership of NATO (Neeps and Tatties
    Organisation)
The heads of The Krankies on Scottish stamps
Signs saying 'English almost spoken' in hotels and
    guesthouses
Claims against the English government for billions
    in back oil revenue
The Isle of Wight demands independence

£250? On Monday!
Oh My Lady Jane

Don't be fooled – ten fancy names for insurance salesmen

Investment consultant
Assurance professional
Savings strategist
Pensions counsellor
Independent broker
Financial adviser
Endowments executive
Contingency specialist
Liquidity planner
Fiscal analyst

Mum, honestly! Ten things parents do which embarrass their children

Kiss them after the age of ten
Sunbathe naked
Take part in the parents' race on sports day
Refuse to take part in the parents' race on sports day
Pick them up from parties
Wave them off at the door when they go on a date
Sit in the room when the latest Madonna video comes on *Top of the Pops*
Complain to shop assistants about the price when they fork out for new trainers
Insist on dancing at their children's parties
Show baby pictures to girlfriends/boyfriends

Junk mail – the case for the defence

It's fun to see so many variations of your surname
It makes the rest of your post seem more interesting
There's something satisfying about throwing away a letter unopened
They're the only letters you don't have to reply to
In a strange way it makes you feel wanted
It keeps Post Office workers off the dole
You never need to buy firelighters
It gives the kids something to cut up
Who else is going to offer you the chance to win £100,000 or a radio alarm clock?
It doesn't matter if it gets lost in the post

Di, first on sports day – honestly

A users' guide to homeopathic remedies

'No additives': *Tastes as bad as it looks*
'Nature's way of stopping pain': *Lethal*
'Pure and gentle': *Can also be used as a soap powder*
'Only natural ingredients': *Gravel from the local quarry*
'Not tested on animals': *It's made from them*
'Gently soothes the system': *Causes diarrhoea*
'Traditional values': *Over-priced*
'Discovered by our ancestors': *When life-expectancy was thirty*
'Life-enhancing': *Well, it can't do you any harm*
'Medically approved': *In Tibet*

Bah, humbug! Ten ways to ruin the Christmas Day spirit

Refuse to wear your paper hat because 'it's silly'
Stay in bed until lunchtime
Insist on watching the subtitled Polish film you got at the video shop
Remind everyone of the calories in a piece of Christmas pudding
Read a book while everyone else plays charades
Refuse to read out the motto from your cracker because it isn't funny
Tell a five-year-old he's too old to believe in Santa Claus
Beat the kids mercilessly at Junior Trivial Pursuit
Say 'Have you still got the receipt?' when you open your main present
Rustle a copy of the *Socialist Worker* during the Queen's Speech

Ten socially aware Christmas presents for the kids

Mineral water pistol
Train enquiry set
Guys and dolls house
Teenage mutant endangered species
Wendy housing association
Action person
Single-parent Happy Families
Recycled rag books
Junior doctor's outfit (to be worn for seventy-two hours at a stretch)
Corgi car with unleaded conversion kit

Tears before bedtime – the ten most common causes of Christmas Day rows

When to open the presents
When to have lunch
When the kids can leave the table to go back to the television
Kids eating an entire selection box by 9 am
Someone using all the tonic water as a soft drink
Children trying to play with each other's toys
Dad being too busy to assemble a complicated toy
Dad interfering in the assembly of a complicated toy
Party poppers used as an offensive weapon
Kisses under the mistletoe which are too passionate

Ten tell-tale signs that Christmas is over

The kids start playing with their old toys again
Television is flooded with holiday ads
The biggest queue in M&S is at the exchange counter
You get a Christmas card from Australia
You're looking forward to going to work
The box of dates is put back in the cupboard for another year
Easter eggs appear in the shops
The house is full of food, but everyone's on a diet
The dustmen refuse to take away the Christmas tree
It's safe to answer unexpected rings at the door

A bit of a do – ten key scenes for the wedding video

The bride's father getting the bill for the reception
The groom the morning after the stag night
Eighty guests fighting for parking space outside the church
The bride's face as her parents do the lambada at the reception
The guests after forty-five minutes of speeches
The vicar being introduced to the happy couple's children
The best man sexually harassing the bridesmaids
The happy couple unwrapping the fourth pop-up toaster in a row
The photographer trying to organise yet another group shot
The best man frantically searching for the ring

'It's only a phase . . . ' ten stages teenagers go through

Looking at their reflection in every shop window they pass
Giving up breakfast
Pretending not to be with the family when on holiday
Being bored with everything
Staying in bed until noon
Keeping a diary
Clothes shopping at jumble sales
Communicating in monosyllables
Displaying an extraordinary talent for secrecy
Going vegetarian

Hold your tongue! Ten things you'll regret saying

If you're ever in Britain, look us up
Yes, I *have* wondered about my relationship with God – come in
If you're really stuck, we can hold the party at my place
I don't mind teaching you to drive
What's everyone having?
Go on, how old do you think I am?
We've got a spare room you could have for a few months
I'm pretty sure I know a short-cut
All right, how much do you want to borrow?
Tell me about it

Oh, the shame of it! Ten things which put you beyond the social pale

Peach-coloured toilet paper in a pampas-green bathroom
Mozart's 20 Golden Greats in your record collection
Routinely refilling a Volvic bottle with tap water
A sign on the toilet door saying 'Here it is!'
Fried breakfasts
Having the car radio tuned to Radio 1
Sliced white bread in the genuine old pine breadbin
A subscription to *Sunday Sport*
Two yards of Shakespeare and Dickens books on your shelves (unopened)
A set of whisky glasses engraved 'Guid health frae bonnie Scotland!'

Not worth buying, even with the free gift

Never-never land: our ten best pieces of advice

Never buy a white car

Never give your telephone number to an insurance salesman

Never agree to 'try something a bit different' at the hairdresser's

Never smoke within a half-mile radius of Sir Clement Freud

Never choose *Good Vibrations* at a karaoke night

Never buy clothes which are a bit tight in the expectation you will lose weight

Never buy a hamburger at a funfair

Never put out the peanuts until your guests arrive

Never go on holiday with friends for longer than a week

Never volunteer

Automania: ten products for the ultimate dream car

Silk festoon windscreen blinds

A glove compartment overflow tank

An alarm which goes off only when someone is trying to steal your car

Traditional pewter steering wheel

Electronic radar-jamming device

Genuine pearl bead seat covers

Security-coded ashtrays

Voice-activated tape with a series of replies to the question: 'Are we nearly there?'

Ejector seat for backseat drivers

Soundproof hood for child's car seat

It's the voice that counts –
Phyllis

Ten new warnings to put on cigarette packets

Smoking can seriously damage your wealth

Smoking can cause you to be banished to the garden at dinner parties

Smoking helps to perpetuate unintelligible ad campaigns

Smoking can result in talking like Phyllis from *Coronation Street*

Smoking increases your dry-cleaning bills

Smoking promotes a golden tan – on your teeth

Smoking provokes health lectures from non-smokers

Smokers suck

Smoking makes you feel guilty

Smoking makes your mouth taste like the bottom of a bird cage

'This is your captain speaking' – a guide to interpretation

'We're just waiting for the last two passengers': *A steward and stewardess have overslept*

'Later on, we'll be serving a light snack': *Peanuts with the drinks*

'For your own comfort, we advise you to keep your seatbelt on': *For our comfort, we don't want you leaving your seat*

'We look forward to you flying with us again soon': *As you've all got return tickets, you haven't got much choice*

'The weather on the ground is cold and rainy': *We're back in the UK*

'Our estimated flying time is two hours': *Plus one hour stacked over Heathrow*

'We seem to have a slight technical hitch': *The in-flight movie is* Skyjacked

'If you look to your left, you should see Paris': *If you don't, we're lost*

'Once we're airborne, I'll be passing through the cabin': *Fielding all those nervous comments about who's flying the plane*

'We hope you had a pleasant flight and that you have a safe onward journey': *I never had to do this public relations guff when I started out*

Danger! Ten things which should carry government health warnings

Vindaloo curries
Mortgage application forms
Skiing holidays
Long-distance coaches
Daytime television
Deckchairs
Five-year-old children
Revolving doors
Letters from the bank
Alex Higgins

School's out for summer – ten tell-tale signs

You can drive to work in half the time
Households all over Britain echo to the refrain: 'Mum, I'm bored'
The kitchen sink is always full
The fridge is always empty
Teachers go silent about their pay and conditions
You suggest a Disney film, they suggest a video of *The Silence of the Lambs*
Every High Street shop has 'Back to School' tableaux from the end of June
There is no escape from Radio 1
You realise, once again, just how expensive it is to keep children amused
The mother's lament makes a comeback: 'It was nice for the first few weeks, but I'll be glad when they go back'

The ten greatest dangers of a federal Europe

Pro-celebrity *boules* on Channel Four
Deep-fried cod and *pommes frites*
No more duty-frees
Pit bull terriers with rabies
Equal airtime on Radio 1 for Charles Aznavour and Johnny Halliday
A half-hour wait for the TV weatherman to get round to your region
Garlic-flavoured crisps
British bobbies carrying sub-machine guns on point duty
Bayern Munich winning the Leyland Daf Cup
The Germans being first on our beaches

The shape of things to come – a guide to our new, cost-effective Armed Forces

The Women's Royal Army Kissogram Corps
The 3rd Armoured Dunstable Brownies
The Sponsored Jumps Parachute Regiment
The Royal Corps of Transport Homestart And Relay Service
The Catering Corps Executive Lunches Division
The Fleet Air Arm Trips-Round-The-Bay Squadron
The Special Air Services Office Security Regiment
The Royal Corps of Signals Telemessage Unit
The Royal Air Force Package Holiday Charter Flights Squadron
Intelligence Corps Industrial Espionage Consultancy

Ten things which lurk beneath the kitchen sink

Enough half-used tins of polish to shine the boots of a regiment

Old knickers and T-shirts which will make 'marvellous dusters'

Half-a-dozen tiles left over from tiling the kitchen walls

A roll of bin liners which didn't fit

Empty coffee and pickle jars which will 'come in useful one day'

A box of solidified Polyfilla

A giant stash of supermarket carrier bags

A cracked saucer and two old Brillo pads

A bottle of stain remover (used once)

A grey dish-cloth with more holes than cloth

Architect-speak – a guide to interpretation

'Traditional': *Heating ducts are on the outside of the building*

'Greenfield site': *Soon to be a grey concrete site*

'Classical': *Giant hangars for DIY retailers*

'We mustn't be afraid of modern designs': *Why doesn't Prince Charles keep his mouth shut?*

'Functional': *You wouldn't catch me living there*

'Street furniture': *Lamp-posts*

'Starter homes': *One up, one down*

'People criticise architecture because it's such a part of their lives': *People are wrong*

'Undoubtedly, mistakes were made in the 60s': *Don't blame me, I was only two at the time*

'Prestige development': *Real bricks*

Ten things to worry about while on holiday

You left the fridge door open

Your cat sits on the doorstep for a fortnight

The council unveils plans for a ring road through your back garden

Your plants die of a broken heart

The burglar alarm rings for ten days

The person who comes in to feed the goldfish rings Australia every day

Free newspapers sprout from your letterbox

Water starts to pour out through the washing machine

Neighbourhood pets discover your cat flap and hold a party in the kitchen

Planning permission is granted to use next door as a mosque

THIS MASTERPIECE OF FUNCTIONAL ARCHITECTURE FOR SALE

Hi! I'm Susie and I go round in circles

Ten divorce dilemmas

Who gets custody of the plants?
Mrs or Ms?
How *do* you divide up a lawnmower?
Should you try to make another go of it
    for the sake of the mortgage?
Will you have to do the census form again?
Who gets stuck with having junk mail
    forwarded?
Do you keep in touch with the in-laws?
Who goes to school plays now?
Dare you sell the wedding ring?
Do you grant visiting rights for the dog?

Be prepared! Ten ways to avoid life's tribulations

Take your own pen to the bank
Take your own toilet paper to the pub
Never book a flight to the continent on bank
    holidays
Get a gas barbecue
Wear earplugs in dentists' waiting rooms
Take your own radio when staying in hotels
Give up supporting West Ham
Rent a video if you're planning to watch TV on
    Saturday night
Have a decent meal before going to a nouvelle
    cuisine restaurant
Pave the garden

Is it a theme pub? Ten tell-tale signs

The bar staff are all resting actors
They serve at least five brands of Peruvian beer
There's a satellite dish outside
The toilets are sign-posted 'Gangsters' and 'Molls'
There are pictures of American baseball stars
    behind the bar
None of the customers is over the age of thirty
They don't sell crisps
There's a three-page cocktail menu
They play Louis Jordan tapes
Your shepherd's pie is served by a man wearing a
    smock and carrying a crook

Ten alternative explanations for corn circles

The steering's gone on the tractor
Somebody's shooting the cover for a *Wishbone
    Ash Greatest Hits* album
A Sinclair C5 veterans' rally
Ramblers desperately looking for the public right
    of way
There's a goat tied up in the middle of the field
The Martians have their own version of *Beadle's
    About*
Drunken droving
Performance artists on holiday
Desperate journalists on a slow news day
A Kellogg's new product development programme

Relationship·speak – a guide to interpretation

'You do love me, don't you?': *You don't love me, do you?*

'We seem to be growing apart': *We're getting fat*

'I'm not prepared to wait forever': *How long are you going to be in that bathroom?*

'We don't communicate anymore': *Switch that damned television off*

'Just because I don't say "I love you" all the time doesn't mean that I don't': *Work that one out*

'I just need a bit of space': *The whole of Britain would do*

'We're too dependent on each other': *You go out with your friends and I'll go out with mine*

'A relationship is something you have to work at': *Like hard labour, really*

'We need to develop our inter-personal skills': *I've learned a lot from* thirtysomething

'You're not as caring as you used to be': *You don't buy me as many presents*

Shrink to fit – a guide to garment labels

'Hand-finished': *Somebody ironed it*

'Wash with care': *Wear once and throw away*

'Tailored': *Tight*

'Cotton enriched': *Polyester with pretensions*

'Dry-clean only': *End up giving more to Sketchley's than you paid for the garment*

'One size fits all': *But fits nobody properly*

'Wash dark colours separately': *This one will run and run*

'Natural fibre': *Full of little knobbly bits*

'Pure silk': *Make sure someone else does the ironing*

'Hand-wash': *Will eventually fit the pet chihuahua*

I've got you at number 3 – and that's my nightmare

Ten nightmares for Mary Whitehouse

Amanda Donohoe in a Dennis Potter play
Bernard Manning on *Jackanory*
A family wedding video directed by Ken Russell
Bret Easton Ellis on *A Book at Bedtime*
Spending a week in Quentin Crisp's New York bedsit
Appearing in a crowd scene in a Madonna video
A Freddy Kruger kissogram
Throwing Damart underwear at Tom Jones
A re-formed Sex Pistols in the *Eurovision Song Contest*
Appearing on the cover of *Forum*

Ten new jobs to cut the dole queue

Nintendo coach
Beadle victim counsellor
Computer virus doctor
Crop circle farmer
Karaoke throat consultant
Virtual reality travel agent
Scottish prime minister
Royal marriage guidance counsellor
Travelling carphone repairman
Satellite dish repo man

FILMS

Oscar ceremony-speak – a guide to interpretation

'I'm speechless': *I can't work without a script*
'Where else could this happen?': *A 65-year-old woman held in by liposuction and a body stocking, wearing a gold lamé dress split to the thigh*
'I don't know where to begin': *No teleprompter*
'I can't believe this is really happening': *Normally, everything I do is pre-recorded*
'A great night for the British film industry': *Another special effects award*
'This is really a tribute to everyone who worked so hard on the picture': *But I've got the award, so there*
'We have to look beyond the narrow world of Hollywood': *Watch out, here comes a political speech*
'Without whom none of this would have been possible': *My plastic surgeon*
'People too numerous to mention': *My ex-husbands*
'A living legend': *Just about living*

Ten films inspired by pop songs

Yellow Submarine (1968): The Beatles
Convoy (1978): C W McCall
Alice's Restaurant (1969): Arlo Guthrie
Harper Valley PTA (1978): Jeannie C Riley
Torn between Two Lovers (1979): Mary MacGregor
Tommy (1975): The Who
Ode to Billy Joe (1976): Bobbie Gentry
The Night the Lights Went Out in Georgia (1981): Vicki Lawrence
Take This Job and Shove It (1981): Johnny Paycheck
Indian Runner (1991): Bruce Springsteen (from the song *Highway Patrolman*)

Darling, I'm speechless – Sir Richard and Anthony

Ten seasonal alternatives to watching *White Christmas*

Santa Claus Conquers the Martians (US, 1964)
Xmas is a Naked Turkey (US, 1911)
Santa Claus is a Louse (France, 1982)
When Santa Rode the Prairie (GB, 1976)
Karl Marx Goes Home for Christmas (US, 1982)
Doc Yak and Santa Claus (US, 1914)
Are You Stone Cold, Santa Claus? (GB, 1977)
Santa and the Ice Cream Bunny (US, 1972)
The Christmas Martian (Canada, 1971)
Andy Williams and the NBC Kids Search for Santa (US, 1985)

Ten working titles of films

Vertigo (1958): From Among the Dead
E.T. (1982): A Boy's Life
Close Encounters of the Third Kind (1977): Watch the Skies
Pretty Woman (1990): Off the Boulevard
Casablanca (1942): Everybody Comes to Rick's
Sunset Boulevard (1950): A Can of Beans
Spellbound (1945): The House of Doctor Edwardes
Ace in the Hole (1951): The Big Carnival
Zelig (1983): The Changing Man
Arachnophobia (1990): Along Came the Spider

Acting funny – ten comedians who have been played by actors

Charlie Chaplin: Robert Downey Jr in *Charlie* (1992)
Tony Hancock: Alfred Molina in *Hancock* (1991)
Bud Flanagan: Roy Hudd in *Underneath the Arches* (1976)
John Belushi: Michael Chiklis in *Wired* (1989)
Buster Keaton: Donald O'Connor in *The Buster Keaton Story* (1956)
Bud Abbott: Harvey Korman in *Bud and Lou* (1978)
Lou Costello: Buddy Hackett in *Bud and Lou* (1978)
W C Fields: Rod Steiger in *W C Fields and Me* (1976)
Lenny Bruce: Dustin Hoffman in *Lenny* (1974)
Groucho Marx: John Bey in *A Day in Hollywood, A Night in the Ukraine* (1979)

Ten star parts that ended up with the second-choice actor (or third, or fourth . . .)

Indiana Jones (Harrison Ford): Tom Selleck
James Bond (Sean Connery): Roger Moore, Richard Burton, Patrick McGoohan
Columbo (Peter Falk): Bing Crosby
Don Corleone in *The Godfather* (Marlon Brando): Laurence Olivier
Michael Corleone (Al Pacino): Warren Beatty, Robert Redford
The *Road to . . .* films (Bob Hope/Bing Crosby): Fred MacMurray/George Burns
Popeye Doyle (Gene Hackman): Jimmy Breslin
Rocky (Sylvester Stallone): James Caan, Burt Reynolds
Superman (Christopher Reeve): Warren Beatty, Robert Redford, Paul Newman, James Caan
Dirty Harry (Clint Eastwood): Frank Sinatra

The write stuff – ten actors who have played novelists

Stacy Keach: Ernest Hemingway in *Hemingway*, 1988
Frederic March: Mark Twain in *The Adventures of Mark Twain*, 1944
Vanessa Redgrave: Agatha Christie in *Agatha*, 1978
Isabelle Adjani: Emily Brontë in *The Brontë Sisters*, 1979
Malcolm McDowell: H G Wells in *Time after Time*, 1979
Christopher Plummer: Rudyard Kipling in *The Man Who Would Be King*, 1975
Richard Chamberlain: F Scott Fitzgerald in *F Scott Fitzgerald and the Last of the Belles*, 1974
Merle Oberon: George Sand in *A Song to Remember*, 1945
Olivia de Havilland: Charlotte Brontë in *Devotion*, 1943
James Mason: Gustave Flaubert in *Madame Bovary*, 1949

Credits where credits are due – a guide to the list at the end of movies

Director: *Man who argues with the producer*

Producer: *Person who checks the cast aren't using too many paper cups*

Scriptwriter: *Someone whose words never actually end up in the movie*

Researcher: *Makes sure nobody drinks Coca-Cola in a costume drama*

Personal Assistant: *Keeps the star sober during shooting*

Musical Director: *Someone with a collection of old hit singles*

Assistant Cinematographer: *Switches off the lights*

Best Boy: *Sent out to buy 35 pizzas and 48 cheeseburgers*

Publicist: *Keeps stories out of the newspapers*

Co-producer: *Producer's wife*

Breathless! Ten films for smokers

The Man Who Would Be King Size
The Life of Briar
Full Metal Smoking Jacket
Flash-the-Ash Gordon
Goodbye, Mr Tips
Crocodile Dunhill
Straw Dog-Ends
Who's Afraid of Virginia Tipped?
The Enigma of Gasper Hauser
The Postman Always Coughs Twice

Ten actors who didn't blow their own horn

Robert De Niro's tenor sax in *New York, New York* (dubbed by Georgie Auld)

James Stewart's trombone in *The Glenn Miller Story* (Joe Yukl)

Richard Gere's cornet in *The Cotton Club* (Warren Vaché)

Forest Whitaker's alto sax in *Bird* (Charlie Parker recordings)

Steve Allen's clarinet in *The Benny Goodman Story* (Benny Goodman)

Kirk Douglas's trumpet in *Young Man with a Horn* (Harry James)

Gene Hackman's tenor sax in *The Conversation* (Justine Gordon)

Paul Newman's trombone in *Paris Blues* (Murray McEachern)

Sidney Poitier's tenor sax in *Paris Blues* (Paul Gonsalves)

Danny Kaye's cornet in *The Five Pennies* (Red Nichols)

The kid's got talent! The ten youngest Oscar winners

Shirley Temple, aged six (1934)
Margaret O'Brien, aged seven (1944)
Vincent Winter, aged seven (1954)
John Whitely, aged nine (1954)
Tatum O'Neal, aged ten (1973)
Claude Jarman Jr, aged twelve (1946)
Bobby Driscoll, aged twelve (1949)
Hayley Mills, aged thirteen (1960)
Patty Duke, aged fourteen (1962)
Deanna Durbin, aged seventeen (1938)

Daddy, will you win an Oscar?
Tatum swots up *Paper Moon*

Seeing double – ten value-for-money Hollywood remakes

Cape Fear is The Key
Robin Hood, Prince of Bicycle Thieves
Edward Scissorhands that Rock the Cradle
Carry On Doctor Zhivago
It's a Mad Mad Mad Mad Max II
Snow White and The Seven Year Itch
Guess Who's Coming to The Naked Lunch
Around The World In 80 Days of Wine and Roses
The Comfort of Strangers on a Train
Citizen Caine Mutiny

From small screen to big screen – ten movie stars who started in sitcoms

Richard Dreyfuss: *Karen* (1964)
Michael J Fox: *Family Ties* (1982–9)
Jamie Lee Curtis: *Operation Petticoat* (1977–8)
Sally Field: *Gidget* (1965–6)
Warren Beatty: *The Many Loves of Dobie Gillis* (1955–9)
Anne Archer: *Bob & Carol & Ted & Alice* (1973–4)
Beau Bridges: *Ensign O'Toole* (1962–3)
Robin Williams: *Mork and Mindy* (1978–82)
Steve Guttenberg: *Billy* (1978–9)
Danny De Vito: *Taxi* (1978–83)

Enter, carrying microphone – ten actors who have played pop stars

Dennis Quaid: Jerry Lee Lewis in *Great Balls of Fire!* (1989)
Lou Diamond Phillips: Ritchie Valens in *La Bamba* (1987)
Val Kilmer: Jim Morrison in *The Doors* (1991)
Jessica Lange: Patsy Kline in *Sweet Dreams* (1985)
Gary Busey: Buddy Holly in *The Buddy Holly Story* (1978)
Gary Oldman: Sid Vicious in *Sid and Nancy* (1986)
Sissy Spacek: Loretta Lynn in *Coal Miner's Daughter* (1980)
Kurt Russell: Elvis Presley in *Elvis: The Movie* (1979)
Mark McGann: John Lennon in *John and Yoko: A Love Story* (1985)
Cynthia Gibb: Karen Carpenter in *The Karen Carpenter Story* (1989)

The first ten films shown on ITV (1955)

A Tale of Five Cities (GB, 1951)
Miracle in Milan (Italy, 1951)
Thunder Rock (GB, 1942)
Ignacé (France, 1937)
Under the Red Robe (GB, 1937)
Dark Journey (GB, 1937)
The First of the Few (GB, 1942)
Candlelight in Algeria (GB, 1943)
Emergency Call (GB, 1952)
The Stars Look Down (GB, 1939)

The first ten films shown on BBC television

The Student of Prague (Germany), screened in 1938
L'Homme du Jour (France), 1938
La Kermesse Héroïque (France), 1938
So Ended a Great Love (Germany), 1938
Deuxième Bureau (France), 1939
Le Patriot (France), 1939
Marie Louise (Switzerland), 1946
Birth of a Nation (USA), 1947
Poil de Carotte (France), 1947
Target for Tonight (GB), 1947

Jamie Lee Curtis, no small frills on the big screen

Playing the PM – Maggie and Robin and Janet and Mike

Ten actors who have played British prime ministers

Ian McShane: Benjamin Disraeli (*Disraeli – Portrait of a Romantic*, 1978)

Robert Donat: William Pitt the Younger (*The Young Mr Pitt*, 1942)

John Mills: George Canning (*Lady Caroline Lamb*, 1972)

Ralph Richardson: William Gladstone (*Khartoum*, 1966)

Simon Ward: Winston Churchill (*Young Winston*, 1972)

Michael Gough: Anthony Eden (*Suez 1956*, 1979)

Peter Barkworth: Stanley Baldwin (*Winston Churchill, the Wilderness Years*, 1981)

Robin Bailey: Neville Chamberlain (*Walk with Destiny*, 1974)

Philip Madoc: David Lloyd George (*The Life and Times of Lloyd George*, 1980)

Janet Brown: Margaret Thatcher (*For Your Eyes Only*, 1981)

Movie shorts – ten names rejected for Snow White's seven dwarfs

Weepy	Lazy
Shirty	Wheezy
Woeful	Shorty
Sniffy	Gloomy
Puffy	Snoopy

Take your partners – ten actresses who danced with Fred Astaire

Joan Crawford (*Dancing Lady*, 1933)

Ginger Rogers (*Top Hat*, 1935)

Eleanor Powell (*Broadway Melody of 1940*, 1940)

Paulette Goddard (*Second Chorus*, 1940)

Rita Hayworth (*You were Never Lovelier*, 1942)

Judy Garland (*Easter Parade*, 1948)

Betty Hutton (*Let's Dance*, 1950)

Vera-Ellen (*Three Little Words*, 1950)

Cyd Charisse (*The Band Wagon*, 1953)

Leslie Caron (*Daddy Long Legs*, 1955)

Ten films that changed the world

The Day the Earth Stood Still (1951)

The Day the World Ended (1956)

The Day the Earth Moved (1974)

Crack in the World (1965)

The Day the Earth Caught Fire (1961)

War of the Worlds (1953)

The Earth Dies Screaming (1964)

When Worlds Collide (1951)

The Day that Shook the World (1977)

It Conquered the World (1956)

A beginners' guide to Rugby Union

'On the blind side': *Effect of post-match booze-up*

'Sidestep': *Manoeuvre to avoid opposing drunks at post-match booze-up*

'Prop': *Device which enables players to stand at the bar all night*

'No. 8': *Regular order along with Nos. 12, 26 and 32 from the Chinese menu*

'Forward pass': *Slurring something suggestive to a team mate's wife*

'Drop kick': *Inevitable result of forward pass*

'Overlap': *Front-row forward's beer gut*

'Scrum': *Freestyle version of queueing at the bar*

'Attempted conversion': *Offering to buy a round of soft drinks*

'Fly half': *A quick one before the game*

First one to drop it
buys the next round

It's a funny old game – ten odd soccer facts

James Gordon of Glasgow Rangers played in all eleven positions for the club between 1910 and 1930

An entire team in Cordoba, Argentina, was jailed in 1972 after the players kicked a linesman to death

Swansea City once had four pairs of brothers on their playing staff at the same time

The entire Southport team was hypnotised before a game against Watford in 1975; they lost 2–1

The goalkeeper of Turkish side Orduspor was given a £50 bonus in 1980 after the team lost 4–0 he normally let in twice that number

Arsenal, Everton and Crystal Palace have all had trawlers named after them

A first-class game has an average of 85 throw-ins, almost one a minute

In 1964, 350 fans died in a riot after an equalising goal for Peru was disallowed in a game against Argentina – 'Anyone can make a mistake,' said the referee

The Liberian national team played against Gambia in 1980 under threat of facing the firing squad if they lost; they drew

Each member of the Kuwait team received a car, a house and £6000 when they qualified for the 1982 World Cup finals

Soccer trials – the top ten footballing hits

Back Home: England (No. 1, 1970)

World in Motion: England with New Order (No. 1, 1990)

This Time (We'll Get it Right): England (No. 2, 1982)

Anfield Rap (Red Machine in Full Effect): Liverpool (No. 3, 1988)

Blue is the Colour: Chelsea (No. 5, 1972)

We Have a Dream: Scotland (No. 5, 1982)

Ossie's Dream (Spurs are on their Way to Wembley): Tottenham Hotspur (No. 5, 1981)

Leeds United: Leeds United (No. 10, 1972)

We All Follow Man United: Manchester United (No. 10, 1985)

Glory, Glory Man United: Manchester United (No. 13, 1983)

Horse nonsense – ten odd facts about the turf

Jockey Frank Hayes died while riding Sweet Kiss in the 1923 Belmont Steeplechase, but still won the race

Emperor Nero gave pensions to retired racehorses and made them dress up in human clothes

American sprinter Jesse Owens beat a racehorse over a 100-yard dash in 1936

The shortest odds ever quoted were 10,000-1 on when Lester Piggott rode Dragon Blood in Milan in 1967

A racehorse averages a speed of 60mph

The first woman to ride in a race was 22-year-old Alicia Meynell in 1804

The oldest jockey was Harry Beasley, who was unplaced in the Corinthian Plate in Ireland in 1935 at the age of 83

The odds against a jump jockey finishing the race seated are 10–1

Elizabeth I went to the races on the eve of the Spanish Armada

Spread Eagle, the 1795 Derby winner, holds the record for covering the most mares in a stud season – 234

'I hit it first time, forsooth . . . ' A soccer XI who sound like thespians

Perry Digweed (Brighton & Hove Albion)
Russell Beardsmore (Manchester United)
Simeon Hodson (West Bromwich Albion)
Bradley Sandeman (Maidstone United)
Spencer Prior (Southend United)
Carlton Palmer (Sheffield Wednesday)
Clayton Blackmore (Manchester United)
Ken De Mange (Hull City)
Matthew Le Tissier (Southampton)
Carlton Fairweather (Wimbledon)
Liburd Henry (Maidstone United)

All in the family – ten footballing brothers

Bryan & Gary Robson (Manchester United/West Bromwich Albion)
John & Justin Fashanu (Wimbledon/Torquay United)
Ron & Peter Springett (QPR)
Bobby & Jack Charlton (Manchester United/ Leeds United)
Ron & Allan Harris (Chelsea/QPR)
Ray & Rodney Wallace (Leeds United)
Paul & Ron Futcher (Grimsby Town/Crewe Alexander)
Allan & Wayne Clarke (Leeds United/Manchester City)
Clive & Bradley Allen (West Ham United/QPR)
Roger & Ian Morgan (QPR)

Ten men who played cricket and soccer for England

Denis Compton (Middlesex and Arsenal)
Harry Makepeace (Lancashire and Everton)
Patsy Hedren (Middlesex and Brentford)
Wally Hardinge (Kent and Sheffield United)
William Gunn (Nottinghamshire and Notts County)
C B Fry (Sussex and Corinthians)
Arthur Milton (Gloucestershire and Arsenal)
Willie Watson (Yorkshire and Huddersfield and Sunderland)
Alfred Lyttelton (Middlesex and Old Etonians)
Andy Ducat (Surrey and Arsenal and Aston Villa)

The boy's done great – the soccer players who went on to manage their clubs

George Graham (Arsenal)
Howard Kendall (Everton)
Billy McNeill (Celtic)
Allan Clarke (Leeds United)
Dave Bassett (Wimbledon)
Terry Venables (Tottenham Hotspur)
Graeme Souness (Liverpool)
Billy Bonds (West Ham)
Gerry Francis (Queen's Park Rangers)
Kevin Keegan (Newcastle United)

Boxing commentator-speak – a guide to interpretation

'A real grudge match': *The pre-fight PR has worked*
'I have to say I'm astonished by the decision': *Puerto Rican judge has been bribed*
'A carefully chosen opponent': *Utterly useless*
'One of British boxing's great characters': *Last seen in a Christmas panto*
'We have great hopes of this boy': *Soon to be seen in panto*
'This is real cat-and-mouse stuff': *Round four and no one's thrown a punch*
'A clash of the Titans': *Two tubs of lard propping each other up*
'A bit ring rusty': *Last fought against Joe Bugner*
'They call this man the Picasso of boxing': *Spends most of his time on the canvas*
'The crowd isn't happy': *Watch out, here come the beer cans*

Joe, making sure there's no rust in his pipes

Boardroom glitz – ten celebrity football club directors

Jim Davidson: Bournemouth (1981–2)
Frank Carson: Colchester United (1987–)
Jasper Carrott: Birmingham City (1979–82)
Tommy Cannon: Rochdale (1986–7)
Sir Richard Attenborough: Chelsea (1969–82)
Bill Kenwright: Everton (1990–)
Charlie Williams: Barnsley (1977–85)
Arthur English: Aldershot (1981–90)
Eric Morecambe: Luton Town (1970–5)
Norman Wisdom: Brighton & Hove Albion
   (1970–8)

The name of the game – ten aptly-named soccer players

Peter Skipper (Wigan)
David Corner (Gateshead)
Nick Marker (Plymouth Argyle)
Steve Ball (Norwich City)
Nicky Cross (Port Vale)
Billy Barr (Halifax Town)
Alan Knill (Bury)
Gary Speed (Leeds United)
Paul Mudd (Scarborough)
Greg Fee (Mansfield Town)

Maradona, getting his kicks

It's a funny old game II – ten quotes from soccer managers

'You're not a real manager unless you've been sacked' (*Malcolm Allison*)

'Some teams are so negative they could be sponsored by Kodak' (*Tommy Docherty*)

'I am a firm believer that if you score one goal the other team have to score two to win' (*Howard Wilkinson*)

'There are only two basic situations in football – either you have the ball or you haven't' (*Ron Greenwood*)

'I promise results, not promises' (*John Bond*)

'Managers get too much of the praise and too much of the blame' (*Sir Alf Ramsey*)

'If you're in the penalty area and aren't sure what to do with the ball, just stick it in the net and we'll discuss your options afterwards' (*Bill Shankly*)

'Women should be in the kitchen, the discotheque and the boutique, but not in football' (*Ron Atkinson*)

'If you win a game you are a genius; if you lose one you are worse than useless. There is no middle road' (*John Toshack*)

'There's no fun in soccer any more . . . we'll end up playing in cemeteries' (*Terry Venables*)

In the penalty box – ten sports stars who have ended up behind bars

Former American light-heavyweight boxing champion *James Scott* was jailed for 30–40 years in 1976 for murder and armed robbery

British 400-metre runner *David Jenkins* served six months of a seven-year sentence in 1988 for conspiracy to smuggle steroids into the USA

Former world heavyweight boxing champion *Sonny Liston* spent five years in prison in the 1940s for robbery with violence

Former Arsenal footballer *Peter Storey* spent twenty-eight days in jail in 1990 for smuggling pornographic videos

Liverpool footballer *Jan Molby* was jailed for three months in 1988 for reckless driving

French cyclist *Eric Ramelet* was jailed for two months in 1987 for drug abuse

Jockey *Lester Piggott* was sentenced to three years in 1987 for tax evasion

Arsenal footballer *Tony Adams* was jailed for four months in 1990 for drink-driving

American Olympic gold medallist *Bob Hayes* served ten months in 1978 for drug smuggling

Footballer *Diego Maradona* was held in custody for thirty-five hours in 1991 before being bailed on charges of drug possession and distribution

When Gooch was a lad – the ten other players in his first Test side

John Edrich

Dennis Amiss

Keith Fletcher

Mike Denness

Tony Greig

Alan Knott

Derek Underwood

Chris Old

John Snow

Geoff Arnold

(The match was against Australia in July 1975, and Gooch scored a duck in both innings)

I'm just a lad in panto, know what I mean, Harry?

Quite remarkable! Captain 'Enery is still a real banger

Quite remarkable! Ten people who have captained teams on *A Question of Sport*

Cliff Morgan
Henry Cooper
Freddie Trueman
Brendan Foster
Bobby Moore
Mary Rand
John Barnes
Gareth Edwards
Willie Carson
Emlyn Hughes

Good sports – ten people who have had sporting venues named after them

Robert Kennedy: the Robert F Kennedy Stadium in Washington DC, home of the Washington Redskins
Bill Shankly: Shankly Gates at Anfield, home of Liverpool FC
Mary Peters: Mary Peters Stadium, Belfast
Jackie Milburn: Jackie Milburn Stand at Newcastle United FC
Denis Compton: Compton Stand at Lord's
Roger Bannister: Roger Bannister Stadium, Harrow
W G Grace: Grace Gate at Lord's
Gary Sobers: Sir Garfield Sobers Pavilion at the Kensington Oval, Barbados
Hubert Humphrey: Hubert Humphrey Metrodome, Minneapolis
Archbishop Makarios: Makarios Stadium, Cyprus

Oh yes they did! Ten sports stars who have appeared in pantomime

Tessa Sanderson (*Aladdin*, 1991)
Frank Bruno (*Robin Hood*, 1991)
Annabel Croft (*Cinderella*, 1991)
Duncan Goodhew (*Aladdin*, 1989)
Ian Botham (*Jack and the Beanstalk*, 1991)
Liz Hobbs (*Robin Hood and the Babes in the Wood*, 1991)
Geoff Capes (*Snow White*, 1991)
Suzanne Dando (*Jack and the Beanstalk*, 1989)
Barry McGuigan (*Snow White*, 1990)
Eddie Kidd (*Aladdin*, 1991)

That's my boy! Ten fathers and sons who played Test cricket

Len and Richard Hutton (England)
Fred and Maurice Tate (England)
Colin and Chris Cowdrey (England)
Mickey and Alec Stewart (England)
Dave and Dudley Nourse (South Africa)
Johnny and Denis Lindsay (South Africa)
George and Ron Headley (West Indies)
Walter and Richard Hadlee (New Zealand)
Lala and Mohinder Armanath (India)
Hanif and Shoaib Mohammad (Pakistan)

Heavy going: 'And this one's my nap for the 3.30' – Andrew

When the going gets heavy . . . an alternative guide for punters

'Soft': *High heels inadvisable*
'Very soft': *Sponsor's marquee sinks in the mud*
'Heavy': *Jockeys issued with life-jackets*
'Very heavy': *RNLI takes over duties of St John Ambulance Brigade*
'Very heavy indeed': *Three-furlong marker becomes three-fathom marker*
'Hard': *Horses have taken a wrong turn on to the main road*
'Very hard': *Horses issued with carpet slippers*
'Firm': *Jockeys put cushions on their saddles*
'Good to firm': *Can't get the marquee poles into the ground*
'Good': *Foreign racecourse*

Sports sponsorship – ten sportsmen and the products they should advertise

Ayrton Senna (laxative tablets)
Dave Bassett (liquorice allsorts)
Will Carling (lager)
Frank Bruno (pipe tobacco)
Ian Bowyer (sausages)
Lance Gibbs (toothpaste)
Rob Andrew (liver salts)
Allan Lamb (New Zealand meat)
Kerry Dixon (electrical goods)
Colin Bell (whisky)

Wicket before legs – a cricket XI which could have been a soccer XI

Tim Robinson (Nottinghamshire): Had trials with Chelsea, Portsmouth and QPR
Wayne Larkins (Durham): Was on Notts County's books
Tony Cottey (Glamorgan): Played for Swansea City
Bill Athey (Gloucestershire): Was offered an apprenticeship by Middlesbrough
Mike Gatting (Middlesex): Had a trial with QPR and was offered an apprenticeship by Watford
Ian Botham (Durham): Played for Scunthorpe United
Neil Burns (Somerset): Schoolboy player with Tottenham Hotspur
Phil Newport (Worcestershire): Had a trial with Southampton
Neil Foster (Essex): Had trials with Ipswich and Colchester
Darren Gough (Yorkshire): Played for Barnsley
Simon Brown (Durham): Offered professional terms with Sunderland

QUOTATIONS

I love me – ten egotistical quotes

'My greatest strength is that I have no weaknesses' (John McEnroe)

'There is no human problem which could not be solved if people would simply do as I advise' (Gore Vidal)

'One of my chief regrets during my years in the theatre is that I could not sit in the audience and watch me' (John Barrymore)

'I never cease to amaze myself. I say this humbly' (Don King)

'I'm one of the world's greatest lovers' (Donny Osmond)

'Destroy me and you destroy the British film industry. Keep me going and I'm the biggest star you've got' (Oliver Reed)

'Team effort is a lot of people doing what I say' (Michael Winner)

'If other people are going to talk, conversation becomes impossible' (James Whistler)

'What the world needs is more geniuses with humility. There are so few of us left' (Oscar Levant)

'There is only one of us in each country' (Bette Davis)

Parting thoughts – ten quotes about death

'For three days after death, hair and fingernails continue to grow, but phone calls taper off' (Johnny Carson)

'On the plus side, death is one of the few things that can be done just as easily lying down' (Woody Allen)

'You don't die in the United States, you underachieve' (Jerzy Kosinski)

'Those who welcome death have only tried it from the ears up' (Walter Mizner)

'You haven't lived until you've died in California' (Mort Sahl)

'Death is the next step after the pension – perpetual retirement without pay' (Jean Giraudoux)

'Since we have to speak well of the dead, let's knock them while they're alive' (John Sloan)

'If I could drop dead right now, I'd be the happiest man alive' (Sam Goldwyn)

'Death comes along like a gas bill one can't pay' (Anthony Burgess)

'A single death is a tragedy, a million deaths is a statistic' (Joseph Stalin)

Anthony Burgess, proof that a choc ice a day keeps the gas man away

'I was misquoted' – what they really said

'If you can't stand the meat, get out of the kitchen' (President Harry S Truman's solution for people without refrigerators)

'Reports of my debt are greatly exaggerated' (Mark Twain on being served with a repossession order)

'I have nothing to offer but Blood Sweat and Tears' (Winston Churchill, confessing to his rather dull record collection)

'I want to be a lawn' (Greta Garbo embracing the Green movement a bit over-enthusiastically)

'Father, I cannot sell a tie' (George Washington pleading not to go into the family business)

'It is peas for our time' (Neville Chamberlain heralding the Common Agricultural Policy)

'We have nothing to lose but our change' (Karl Marx on his way to the slot-machine arcade)

'Life's too short to staff a classroom' (Shirley Conran on the crisis in education)

'In the future, everyone will be Amos for 15 minutes' (Andy Warhol predicting a massive revival of *Amos 'n' Andy*)

'I have nothing to declare except my jeans' (Oscar Wilde taking a suitcase full of Levi's to Russia)

Lost in thought – ten quotes about philosophy

'I've developed a new philosophy – I only dread one day at a time' (Charles M Schulz)

'There is no record in human history of a happy philosopher' (H L Mencken)

'Philosophy is common sense in a dress suit' (Oliver S Braston)

'I don't think about deep things – if you can't take a bite out of it, it doesn't exist' (Ted Nugent)

'Philosophers are adults who persist in asking childish questions' (Sir Isaiah Berlin)

'Philosophers are intellectual troublemakers' (A J Ayer)

'Science is what you know, philosophy is what you don't know' (Bertrand Russell)

'My advice to you is not to inquire why or whither, but just enjoy your ice-cream while it's on your plate – that's my philosophy' (Thornton Wilder)

'Philosophy teaches us to bear with equanimity the misfortunes of others' (Oscar Wilde)

'Philosophy is language idling' (Ludwig von Wittgenstein)

'Rumours of my wit have been greatly exaggerated': ten Mark Twain quotes

'Life would be infinitely happier if we could only be born at the age of eighty and gradually approach eighteen'

'Familiarity breeds contempt – and children'

'Cauliflower is nothing but cabbage with a college education'

'Man is the only animal that blushes – or needs to'

'If you tell the truth you don't have to remember anything'

'A flea can be taught everything a congressman can'

'Good breeding consists in concealing how much we think of ourselves and how little we think of the other person'

'Fewer things are harder to put up with than the annoyance of a good example'

'When angry, count four; when very angry, swear'

'It takes your enemy and your friend, working together, to hurt you to the heart; the one to slander you and the other to get the news to you'

Hook lines – ten quotes about fishing

'Fishing is a laborious way of taking it easy
   (Franklin P Jones)
'Old fishermen don't die – they just smell that way'
   (Anon)
'Fishing, with me, has always been an excuse to
   drink in the daytime' (Jimmy Cannon)
'Angling may be said to be so like the
   mathematics, that it can never be fully learnt'
   (Izaak Walton)
'Truth is when one fisherman calls another
   fisherman a liar' (Anon)
'The trouble with fish is that they go on holiday the
   same time most anglers do' (Anon)
'Fishing is a delusion entirely surrounded by liars
   in old clothes' (Don Marquis)
'How far an angler will stretch the truth depends
   on how far he can stretch his arms' (Anon)
'The charm of fishing is that it is the pursuit of
   what is elusive but obtainable, a perpetual series
   of occasions for hope' (John Buchan)
'Maybe the fish goes home and brags about the
   size of the bait he stole' (Anon)

Ten quotes to ponder under the mistletoe

'The first kiss is stolen by the man; the last is
   begged by the woman' (H L Mencken)
'Marriage is the miracle that transforms a kiss from
   a pleasure into a duty' (Helen Rowland)
'I wasn't kissing her, I was whispering in her
   mouth' (Chico Marx)
'There is always one who kisses and one who only
   allows the kiss' (George Bernard Shaw)
'Whoever named it necking was a poor judge of
   anatomy' (Groucho Marx)
'Kissing don't last; cookery do!' (George
   Meredith)
'I am in favour of preserving the French habit of
   kissing ladies' hands – after all, one must start
   somewhere' (Sacha Guitry)
If you are ever in doubt as to whether or not you
   should kiss a pretty girl, always give her the
   benefit of the doubt' (Thomas Carlyle)
Few men know how to kiss well; fortunately, I've
   always had time to teach them' (Mae West)
'You have to kiss an awful lot of frogs before you
   find a prince' (Anon)

First, close your eyes . . . – Mae

Marching to a different drummer – ten pearls of wisdom from Bob Dylan

'I would like to do something worthwhile, like maybe plant a tree on the ocean'

'Art, if there is such a thing, is in the bathrooms – everybody knows that'

'All my records are comedy records'

'I don't call myself a poet because I don't like the word – I'm a trapeze artist'

'I've done more for Dylan Thomas than he's done for me'

'Folk singing is just a bunch of fat people'

'I don't have anything but darkness to lose'

'Bob Dylan has always been here – always was. When I was a child there was Bob Dylan'

'I'm just the postman, I deliver the songs'

'I've been wearing black leather all my life'

Maggie's out – Bob bought the farm instead

Rural gibes – ten quotes about the countryside

'That's the trouble with the country – there's too much public world between the private ones' (Dylan Thomas)

'I have never understood why anybody agreed to go on being a rustic after about 1400' (Kingsley Amis)

'The country has charms only for those not obliged to stay there' (Edouard Manet)

'I am at two with nature' (Woody Allen)

'I'm not the type who wants to go back to the land; I am the type who wants to go back to the hotel' (Fran Lebowitz)

'Anybody can be good in the country; there are no temptations there' (Oscar Wilde)

'There is nothing good to be had in the country, or, if there be, they will not let you have it' (William Hazlitt)

'I loathe the country and everything that relates to it' (William Congreve)

'It is pure unadulterated country life – they get up early because they have so much to do and go to bed early because they have so little to think about' (Oscar Wilde)

'The chicken is the country's, but the city eats it' (George Herbert)

Fighting talk – ten quotes about boxing

'First your legs go. Then your reflexes go. Then your friends go' (Willie Pep)

'A boxer is a round peg in a square ring, manipulated by others for profit' (Ronald Bergan)

'A lot of boxing promoters couldn't match the cheeks of their own backside' (Mickey Duff)

'Boxing is the best and most individual lifestyle you can have in society without being a criminal' (Randy Neumann)

'Boxing is not a sport, it's a criminal activity' (Ernst Jokl)

'Boxing is sort of like jazz – the better it is, the fewer people can understand it' (George Foreman)

'All fighters are prostitutes and all promoters are pimps' (Larry Holmes)

'This is the only sport in the world where two guys get paid for doing something they'd be arrested for if they got drunk and did it for nothing' (Paul Stewart)

'There's got to be good guys and there's got to be bad guys. That's what the people pay for, to see the bad guys get beat' (Sonny Liston)

'Age is a mighty important subject for a boxing champion, because it is the one opponent he can't lick' (Wilfrid Diamond)

All in the eyes – Diamond-hunter Joan, Dame Edna and Twiggy

Notional health service – ten quotes about taking care of yourself

'The only reason I would take up jogging is so that I could hear heavy breathing again' (Erma Bombeck)

'Exercise is bunk. If you are healthy, you don't need it: if you are sick, you shouldn't take it' (Henry Ford)

'I have always said that exercise is a short cut to the cemetery' (John Mortimer)

'I like long walks, especially when they are taken by people who annoy me' (Fred Allen)

'If God wanted us to bend over, he'd put diamonds on the floor' (Joan Rivers)

'Early to rise and early to bed makes a male healthy, wealthy and dead' (James Thurber)

'Little good can come of regular exercise which reduces life to a monotonous machine' (E V Knox)

'Too much health is unhealthy' (Leo Rosten)

'The true index of a man's character is the health of his wife' (Cyril Connolly)

'There is no human activity – eating, sleeping, drinking or sex – which some doctor somewhere won't discover leads directly to cardiac arrest' (John Mortimer)

Money, money, money

'Money is like manure – you have to spread it around or it smells' (John Paul Getty)

'Money is the poor man's credit card' (Marshall McLuhan)

'I have a strange affinity with money. I make it and spend it' (Cher)

'Money can't buy happiness, but it can buy the kind of misery you prefer' (Hobart Brown)

'Money brings some happiness, but after a certain point it just brings more money' (Neil Simon)

'True, you can't take it with you, but then that's not the place where it comes in handy' (Brendan Francis)

'If you would know what the Lord God thinks of money, you only have to look at those to whom He gives it' (Maurice Baring)

'Those that have some think the most important thing in the world is love. The poor know it is money' (Gerald Brenan)

'If you can actually count your money, then you are not a really rich man' (John Paul Getty)

'Money is good for bribing yourself through the inconveniences of life' (Gottfried Reinhardt)

Dress sense – ten quotes about fashion

'Your right to wear a mint-green polyester leisure suit ends where it meets my eye' (Fran Lebowitz)

'A dress has no meaning unless it makes a man want to take it off' (Françoise Sagan)

'Haute couture should be fun, foolish and almost unwearable' (Christian Lacroix)

'Never wear anything that panics the cat' (P J O'Rourke)

'The surest way to be out of fashion tomorrow is to be in the forefront of it today' (Derek Marlowe)

'Fashion is what one wears oneself. What is unfashionable is what other people wear' (Oscar Wilde)

'It is not pansy to be elegant, just as it is not elegant to be pansy' (Hardy Amies)

'To call a fashion wearable is the kiss of death – no new fashion worth its salt is ever wearable' (Eugenia Sheppard)

'Fashion can be bought – style one must possess' (Edna Woolman Chase)

'Her hat is a creation that will never go out of style. It will look just as ridiculous year after year' (Fred Allen)

All in the mind – ten quotes about psychiatry

'A psychiatrist is a fellow who asks you a lot of expensive questions your wife asks you for nothing' (Joey Adams)

'A psychiatrist is the next man you start talking to after you start talking to yourself' (Fred Allen)

'Psychiatry: the care of the id by the odd' (Anon)

'Anybody who goes to see a psychiatrist ought to have his head examined' (Sam Goldwyn)

'A psychiatrist is a man who goes to the Folies-Bergère and looks at the audience' (Mervyn Stockwood)

'Psychoanalysis is confession without absolution' (G K Chesterton)

'Psychiatry's chief contribution to philosophy is the discovery that the toilet is the seat of the soul' (Alexander Chase)

'Psychiatry enables us to correct our faults by confessing our parents' shortcomings' (Laurence Peter)

'If you talk to God you are praying. If God talks to you, you have schizophrenia' (Thomas Szasz)

'A neurotic is a person who builds a castle in the air. A psychotic is the person who lives in it. A psychiatrist is the person who collects the rent' (Jerome Lawrence)

Fashionable Fergie – very feline

Ten quotes about rock stars

'Elvis Presley had the whole world in his hand and he put it in the lavatory' (Screaming Lord Sutch)

'Bob is Bob, and he always will be. And that's why he's Bob' (Jeff Lynne on Bob Dylan)

'Frank Zappa couldn't write a decent song if you gave him a million and a year on an island in Greece' (Lou Reed)

'If a horse could sing in a monotone, the horse would sound like Carly Simon' (Robert Christgau)

'Madonna is so hairy, when she lifted her arm I thought it was Tina Turner in her armpit' (Joan Rivers)

'The only man to live in a G-Plan castle' (Jimmy Page on Bill Wyman)

'U2 are simple though, aren't they? My window cleaner's got more to say' (Mark E Smith)

'Jerry Lee Lewis is an individual and he is Jerry Lee Lewis and there will never be another talent like Jerry Lee Lewis' (Jerry Lee Lewis)

'He moves like a parody between a majorette girl and Fred Astaire' (Truman Capote on Mick Jagger)

'A New Age nightmare . . . a bald-headed banshee' (Richard Blackwell on Sinead O'Connor)

Brevity is the soul of repartee – ten replies you wish you'd thought of

Oscar Wilde: 'It's a pretty poor work of art'
James Whistler: 'Yes. And you're a pretty poor work of nature'

George Bernard Shaw: 'Isn't it true, my dear, that male judgement is superior to female judgement?'
Mrs Shaw: 'Of course, dear. After all, you married me and I you'

Bessie Braddock: 'Winston, you're drunk!'
Winston Churchill: 'Bessie, you're ugly. But tomorrow morning I shall be sober'

Convicted criminal: 'As God is my judge – I am innocent'
Judge Norman Birkett: 'He isn't; I am, and you're not!'

Clare Booth Luce (opening a door): 'Age before beauty'
Dorothy Parker (going through first): 'Pearls before swine'

Singer: 'You know, my dear, I insured my voice for fifty thousand dollars'
Miriam Hopkins: 'That's wonderful. And what did you do with the money?'

Sir Lewis Morris: 'The press are neglecting my poems. It is a conspiracy of silence. What ought I to do Oscar?'
Oscar Wilde: 'Join it!'

Jacob Epstein: 'Do you remember the days before we knew each other?'
Mark Gertler: 'Yes'
Jacob Epstein: 'Well then, let's go back to them'

George Bernard Shaw: 'Am reserving two tickets for you for my première. Come and bring a friend – if you have one'
Winston Churchill: 'Impossible to be present for the first performance. Will attend the second – if there is one'

Actor: 'Last night I was a sensation at the Roxy. I had the audience glued to their seats'
George Jessel: 'How clever of you to think of it'

Frank – it's all Greek to me, claims Lou

Gore blimey – ten quotes from Mr Vidal

'A narcissist is someone better looking than you are'

'Never have children, only grandchildren'

'Whenever a friend succeeds, a little something in me dies'

'Television is now so desperately hungry for material that they're scraping the top of the barrel'

'I'm all for bringing back the birch – but only between consenting adults'

'A good deed never goes unpunished'

'Any American who is prepared to run for president should automatically, by definition, be disqualified from ever doing so'

'Commercialism is doing well that which should not be done at all'

'The aim of so much journalism is to exploit the moral prejudices of the reader, to say nothing of those of the proprietor'

'Never miss a chance to have sex or appear on television'

Ten quotes about elections

'During an election campaign the air is full of speeches – and vice versa' (Henry Adams)

'Voters do not decide issues – they decide who will decide issues' (George Will)

'If voting changed anything, they'd make it illegal' (Anon)

'A manifesto is issued to get votes and is not to be taken as gospel' (Lord Denning)

'Bad officials are elected by good citizens who do not vote' (George Nathan)

'Democracy substitutes election by the incompetent many for appointment by the corrupt few' (George Bernard Shaw)

'Elections are won by men and women chiefly because most people vote against somebody rather than for somebody' (Franklin P Adams)

'A politician thinks of the next election, a statesman thinks of the next generation' (James Freeman Clarke)

'It was not a defeat – I was merely placed third in the polls' (Bill Pitt, Liberal candidate)

'Landslides, on the whole, don't produce successful governments' (Francis Pym)

Press counsel – ten views of journalism

'The secret of successful journalism is to make your readers so angry they will write half your paper for you' (C E M Joad)

'Journalism is organised gossip' (Edward Egglestone)

'Journalism largely consists of saying "Lord Jones Dead" to people who never knew Lord Jones was alive' (G K Chesterton)

'The only qualities for real success in journalism are ratlike cunning, a plausible manner and a little literary ability' (Nicholas Tomalin)

'Facing the press is more difficult than bathing a leper' (Mother Teresa)

'Newspapers are unable, seemingly, to discriminate between a bicycle accident and the collapse of civilisation' (George Bernard Shaw)

'When a journalist enters the room, your privacy ends and his begins' (Warren Beatty)

'Journalists write because they have nothing to say, and have something to say because they write' (Karl Kraus)

'Journalism – an ability to meet the challenge of filling the space' (Dame Rebecca West)

'The Press is easier squashed than squared' (Sir Winston Churchill)

MUSIC

A beginner's guide to music

Jazz: *Five men on the same stage all playing a different tune*

Blues: *Played exclusively by people who woke up this morning*

World music: *A dozen different types of percussion going at once*

Opera: *People singing when they should be talking*

Rap: *People talking when they should be singing*

Classical: *Discover the forty-five minutes they left out of the TV ad*

Folk: *Endless songs about shipwrecks in the nineteenth century*

Big band: *Twenty men who take it in turns to stand up, plus a drummer*

Heavy metal: *Codpiece and chaps*

House music: *OK as long as it's not the house next door*

Sing something stupid – ten memorable song titles

All I Want for Christmas Is a Dukla Prague Away Kit (Half Man Half Biscuit)

Dark Side of the Sausage (Christ & Satan)

The Pencil Was Obviously Sharpened by a Left-Handed Indian Knife Thrower (Claim)

Slimy Cod in a Toaster (KSMB)

Grandma Got Run Over by a Reindeer (Elmo & Patsy)

Sumo Lawnmower and His Inescapable Trap of Doom (Lawnmower Deth)

Theme From an Imaginary Midget Western (Adrenalin OD)

Never Do a Tango With an Eskimo (Alma Cogan)

Let's Go Gas Board, Punch Official (Sore Throat)

Our Dog Ate My Vomit (Diced Carrots)

Cod and chaps – Pat and Roger's guide to heavy metal

Charlie, undercover man

No job description required – Phil Collins

Crock 'n' roll – ten numbers for the next Rolling Stones tour

Street Fighting Gran
Gimme Sheltered Accommodation
Fade Away
Let's Spend the Evening Together
Paint it Magnolia
(I Can't Get No)
Time is not on My Side
Undercover of the Nightshirt
Start Me Up – Please
I Wanna be your Nan

Ten new categories for the BRIT Awards

Best Use of Phil Collins
Best Group Performing All Its Own Vocals
Most Convincing Mime Artists
Most Outstanding Contribution to Charity
    Concerts
Furthest Distance Travelled to Record an Album
Most Original Hairstyle
Most Pretentious Dedication on a Record Sleeve
Lifetime Achievement Award (open to anyone
    over the age of 25)
Least Promising Newcomer
The Rolling Stones Gold Watch Award

Keith – don't be afraid

Beatlemania – ten people who chose the Fab Four on *Desert Island Discs*

David Owen: *Lucy in the Sky with Diamonds*
Keith Floyd: *Hey Jude*
Cilla Black: *The Long and Winding Road*
Vera Lynn: *Till There Was You*
Ian Botham: *Yesterday*
Lord King: *She's Leaving Home*
Barbara Castle: *Love Me Do*
Anita Dobson: *Please Please Me*
The Duchess of Kent: *Maxwell's Silver Hammer*
David Essex: *In My Life*

Sing something seasonal – ten updated Christmas carols

Hark the Harlem Angel Raps
Away in a Mazda
I Saw Three Ships A-Whaling
In the Bleak Midwinter Mini-Break
We Three King's Singers
I Arrest Ye Merry Gentlemen
While Shepherds Watched their Stocks and Shares
The Holly and the Ivory
Violent Night
Once in Viscount Linley's City

Political broadcasts – number one records at the last ten general elections

Stay: Shakespears Sister, April 1991
I Wanna Dance with Somebody (Who Loves Me): Whitney Houston, June 1987
Every Breath You Take: The Police, June 1983
Bright Eyes: Art Garfunkel, May 1979
Kung Fu Fighting: Carl Douglas, October 1974
Devil Gate Drive: Suzi Quatro, February 1974
In the Summertime: Mungo Jerry, June 1970
The Sun Ain't Gonna Shine Any More: The Walker Brothers, March 1966
Oh Pretty Woman: Roy Orbison, October 1964
Only Sixteen: Craig Douglas, October 1959

If Phillip Schofield can do it . . . ten musical productions for deejays

Not 'Arfa Sixpence (Alan Freeman)
Guys and Gals (Jimmy Savile)
Man of La Manchester (Dave Lee Travis)
One Guy Named Mayo (Simon Mayo)
An American in the Paris Studios (Paul Gambaccini)
A Star is Gorn (Derek Jameson)
My Fair Laddie (Nicky Campbell)
Strike up the Indie Label Band (John Peel)
Thoroughly Modern Wally (Gary Davies)
Aspects of Hove (any Radio Brighton presenter)

Happy days for the queen of rock – Suzi

Rock stars who started their own record labels

Paul Weller (Respond)
Elton John (Rocket Records)
The Beach Boys (Brother Records)
The Buzzcocks (New Hormones)
The Rolling Stones (Rolling Stones Records)
UB40 (DEP International)
The Beatles (Apple)
The Pogues (Pogue Mahone)
Dave Stewart (Anxious Records)
Madness (Zarjazz)

Elton, a real take-off

Star turns – ten singers who have guested on TV shows

Leonard Cohen (*Miami Vice*)
Ray Charles (*Moonlighting*)
Dionne Warwick (*The Rockford Files*)
Boy George (*The A-Team*)
Carly Simon (*thirtysomething*)
Suzi Quatro (*Happy Days*)
David Bowie (*Dream On*)
Bill Medley (*Cheers*)
Smokey Robinson (*Generations*)
Sheena Easton (*Miami Vice*)

A plain man's guide to classical music

Bach: *The sound a dog makes*
Offenbach: *The sound two dogs make*
Debussy: *The thing you catch to worky*
Conductor: *Collects de fare on debussy*
Pizzicato: *Same as Brahms and Liszt*
String Quartet: *Lady Penelope, Parker, Scott and Virgil*
Purcell: *Washes whiter*
Ravel's *Bolero*: *A new style of shoe*
Rossini: *Lead singer in Status Quo*
Carl Orff: *That bloke in the old horror films*

Where ten pop groups found their names

T'Pau: From a Vulcan character in *Star Trek*
Right Said Fred: From a 1962 hit by Bernard Cribbins
Clannad: 'Clannad' is Gaelic for family
Simple Minds: From the lyrics of the David Bowie song *Jean Genie*
Lynyrd Skynyrd: From the band members' school gym teacher, Leonard Skinner
Duran Duran: The name of a character in *Barbarella*
The Stone Roses: An amalgam of a Jam song, *English Rose*, and the group's favourite band, The Rolling Stones
Level 42: From *The Hitch-Hiker's Guide to the Galaxy*, in which '42' is the answer to everything
Iron Maiden: A medieval torture device
Art of Noise: From an Italian futurist manifesto

Lost for words – ten snappy song titles

Why (Carly Simon, 1982)
When (Showaddywaddy, 1977)
Wot (Captain Sensible, 1982)
Cry (Godley & Creme, 1985)
Bad (Michael Jackson, 1987)
She (Charles Aznavour, 1974)
Him (Sarah Brightman, 1983)
If (Telly Savalas, 1975)
Yep (Duane Eddy, 1959)
Till (Tom Jones, 1971)

Cover versions – ten pseudonyms used by rock stars

Blind Boy Grunt (Bob Dylan)
Dr Winston O'Boogie (John Lennon)
Nanker and Phelge (Mick Jagger and Keith Richards)
L'Angelo Mysterioso (George Harrison)
Larry Lurex (Freddie Mercury)
Bernard Webb (Paul McCartney)
Camille (Prince)
Lefty Wilbury (Roy Orbison)
Eivets Rednow (Stevie Wonder)
The Imposter (Elvis Costello)

Alvin's Buddy – Oh Boy

Tune that name – pop stars immortalised in song

Madonna, Sean and Me (Sonic Youth)
Joe Strummer's Wallet (The Stingrays)
John, Paul, George and Ringo (The Bulldogs)
I Feel Like Buddy Holly (Alvin Stardust)
Ode to Otis Redding (Mark Johnson)
Elvis Presley and America (U2)
Dolly Parton's Guitar (Lee Hazlewood)
Jackie Wilson Said (Van Morrison)
The Story of Bo Diddley (The Animals)
The Night Hank Williams Came to Town (Johnny Cash)

Ten records that were guaranteed airtime

Radio Radio (Elvis Costello)
Radio Waves (Roger Waters)
On My Radio (The Selecter)
Radio Gaga (Queen)
Capital Radio (The Clash)
Turn Your Radio On (Ray Stevens)
Radio Song (REM)
Radio Romance (Tiffany)
Radio Head (Talking Heads)
Radio Heart (Radio Heart & Gary Numan)

Bowie's all the buzz, honey

The seal of success – ten records banned by the BBC

Young and Healthy (Bing Crosby, 1934)
The Man with the Golden Arm (Eddie Calvert, 1956)
Eve of Destruction (Barry McGuire, 1965)
Je T'Aime . . . Moi Non Plus (Jane Birkin and Serge Gainsbourg, 1969)
Up Je T'Aime (Frankie Howerd and June Whitfield, 1970)
You're Breaking my Heart (Harry Nilsson, 1972)
God Save the Queen (The Sex Pistols, 1977)
Too Drunk To **** (Dead Kennedys, 1981)
Relax (Frankie Goes To Hollywood, 1983)
Xaviera!! (Xaviera Hollander, 1977)

Ten rock stars who went to public school

Peter Gabriel (Charterhouse)
Shane McGowan (Westminster)
Stewart Copeland (Millfield)
Chris De Burgh (Marlborough)
Mick Fleetwood (Sherborne)
Bruce Dickinson (Oundle)
David Dundas (Harrow)
Chris Lowe (Arnold)
Tom Robinson (Friends' Saffron Walden)
Ian Anderson (King Edward VII, Lytham)

Crooner Chris, everyone's favourite old boy

When we were young – ten rock stars' former groups

Mick Hucknall (The Frantic Elevators)
Roland Gift (Acrylic Victims)
David Bowie (The King Bees)
Joe Jackson (Arms and Legs)
Eric Clapton (Casey Jones and the Engineers)
Van Morrison (Deanie Sands and the Javelins)
Paul Young (Kat Kool and the Kool Kats)
Mark Knopfler (Brewer's Droop)
Holly Johnson (Hollycaust)
Adam Ant (Bazooka Joe and his Rhythm Hot Shots)

The first ten singles to sell a million in the UK

Laughing Song (Bert Shepard, 1910)
Cohen on the Telephone (Joe Hayman, 1914)
Oh for the Wings of a Dove (Ernest Lough, 1927)
Wedding Samba (Edmundo Ros, 1949)
Harry Lime Theme (Anton Karas, 1950)
Charmaine (Mantovani, 1951)
Wyoming (Mantovani, 1951)
Black and White Rag (Winifred Atwell, 1952)
Auf Wiedersehen Sweetheart (Vera Lynn, 1952)
Yours (Vera Lynn, 1952)

If music be the food of love, don't listen to this lot

I Wanna Sex You Up: Color Me Badd (1991)
I Want Your Sex: George Michael (1987)
Sex Over the Phone: Village People (1985)
The Sex of It: Kid Creole and the Coconuts (1989)
Sex Talk (Live): T'Pau (1988)
People are Still Having Sex: Latour (1991)
XX Sex: We've got a Fuzzbox and We're gonna Use It (1986)
Get Up I feel like being a Sex Machine: James Brown (1970)
Let's Talk About Sex: Salt 'N' Pepa (1991)
I'm Too Sexy: Right Said Fred (1991)

Look what they've done to our song — ten pulverised pop classics

Heartbreak Hotel: Stan Freberg (1956)
(I Can't Get No) Satisfaction: Bubblerock (1974)
Love Me Tender: Roland Rat (1984)
Wild Thing: The Goodies (1975)
Summer Holiday: Kevin the Gerbil (1984)
Nights in White Satin: The Dickies (1979)
A Hard Day's Night: Peter Sellers (1965)
You've Lost that Loving Feeling: Telly Savalas (1975)
White Christmas: Keith Harris and Orville (1985)
Bohemian Rhapsody: Bad News (1987)

Ten songs they should use in bank commercials

Don't Believe a Word: Thin Lizzy
Get the Balance Right: Depeche Mode
Even the Bad Times are Good: The Tremeloes
Money's Too Tight (To Mention): Simply Red
Every Day Hurts: Sad Café
I.O.U.: Freeez
The Land of Make Believe: Buck's Fizz
Rat Trap: The Boomtown Rats
Giving it All Away: Roger Daltrey
Money That's Your Problem: Tonight

George, still not satisfied

Ciao, Paul Gambaccini, about my platter . . .

Ten cover versions we're waiting for

Anyway Anyhow Anywhere (Madonna)
Does Your Mother Know (Bill Wyman)
Another Funny Honeymoon (Rod Stewart)
It's the Same Old Song (Status Quo)
It's All Over Now (Elaine Page)
Too Much Too Young (New Kids On The Block)
Bend Me Shape Me (Michael Jackson)
Yummy Yummy Yummy (Luciano Pavarotti)
Like a Virgin (Cliff Richard)
A Walk in the Black Forest (Sting)

No messing – ten records that went straight to No. 1

Jailhouse Rock: Elvis Presley (1958)
The Young Ones: Cliff Richard and the Shadows (1962)
Get Back: The Beatles (1969)
Cum on Feel the Noize: Slade (1973)
I Love You Love Me Love: Gary Glitter (1973)
Don't Stand so Close to Me: The Police (1980)
Two Tribes: Frankie Goes To Hollywood (1984)
Do They Know It's Christmas?: Band Aid (1984)
Sealed with a Kiss: Jason Donovan (1989)
Do They Know It's Christmas?: Band Aid II (1989)

The sausage top ten

Boom-Banger-Banger
Another Prick in the Wall's
I've Got You under my Skinless
Frankfurter and Johnny
Sgt Pepperoni's Lonely Hearts Club Band
How Much is that Hot Doggy in the Window?
The Wurst Part of Breaking Up
Saveloy your Kisses for Me
Keep Right on Till the End of the Toad (in the Hole)
Winter Cumberland

The first ten singles to top the British charts (1952–3)

Here in my Heart (Al Martino)
You belong to Me (Jo Stafford)
Comes A-Long A-Love (Kay Starr)
Outside of Heaven (Eddie Fisher)
Don't let the Stars get in your Eyes (Perry Como)
She Wears Red Feathers (Guy Mitchell)
Broken Wings (Stargazers)
(How Much Is) That Doggie in the Window (Lita Roza)
I Believe (Frankie Laine)
I'm Walking behind You (Eddie Fisher)

But they probably love their mums – ten classic heavy metal albums

Filth Hounds of Hades (Tank)
Scumdogs of the Universe (GWAR)
If you Want Blood you've got It (AC/DC)
Annihilation of Civilisation (Evil Dead)
Pure Filth (Warfare)
See you in Hell (Grim Reaper)
Live Evil (Black Sabbath)
Blood, Fire, Death (Bathory)
Devil's Victim (Dark Wizard)
Weapon Monster (Samurai)

Songs for Sunday traders

Let It B&Q
Deep in the Heart of Texas Homecare
The Safeway We Were
MFI who have Nothing
The Green Green Grass of Homebase
Do-It-All Again
In an English Country Garden Centre
Jesus Christ Superstore
Cash 'n' Carry that Weight
Bed Sales in the Sunset

The sincerest form of flattery – ten rock acts based on the real thing

Bjorn Again (Abba)
Dread Zeppelin (Led Zeppelin)
The Joshua Trio (U2)
The Men in Black (The Stranglers)
The Counterfeit Stones (The Rolling Stones)
Kween (Queen)
Elton Jack (Elton John)
The Australian Doors (The Doors)
Liberty Mountain (Elvis Presley)
The Bootleg Beatles (The Beatles)

Hot hits – ten songs they should play in Indian restaurants

Stand by your Nan (Tammy Wynette)
Tikka to Ride (The Beatles)
It's my Chappati (Lesley Gore)
Pappadum Preach (Madonna)
Korma Chameleon (Culture Club)
Bhaji Bhaji (Gladys Knight and the Pips)
Vindaloo (Abba)
Another Day of Pilau Rice (Phil Collins)
Chutney's in Love (Rickie Lee Jones)
Raitha said Fred (Bernard Cribbins)

The first ten albums to top the British charts

South Pacific (Film Soundtrack), 1958
The Explosive Freddy Cannon (Freddy Cannon), 1960
Elvis is Back (Elvis Presley), 1960
Down Drury Lane to Memory Lane (101 Strings), 1960
GI Blues (Elvis Presley), 1961
Black and White Minstrel Show (George Mitchell Minstrels), 1961
The Shadows (Shadows), 1961
21 Today (Cliff Richard), 1961
Another Black and White Minstrels Show (George Mitchell Minstrels), 1961
Blue Hawaii (Elvis Presley), 1962

Madonna, Frying Pan Alley Girl

It's where the buffalo roam, ho, ho – Paul

Mix and match – ten new TV shows to brighten up the schedules

'The Coronation Game': A pint at the Rovers Return, a family bust-up, then two minutes to make a pizza base

'You've Been Highwayed': Embarrassing videos of people caught singing hymns with Sir Harry Secombe

'Blind Trek': Essex girl wins glass-blowing weekend with a Klingon

'Cagney and Greavsie': Meaningful women's talk in the changing rooms at West Ham

'The Food and Drink Blockbusters': 'I'd like a pea please, Bob'

'Vic Reeves Big Crimewatch': Man sought after a vicious attack with a sausage

'The Darling Buds of Beadle': Pop Larkin is confronted by a 'council official' who claims there's a demolition order on his sideburns

'Inspector Who': Time-travelling policeman solves murders from a police box in Oxford

'It'll be Alright on the News at Ten': Newsreader spends entire programme saying 'We don't seem to be able to bring you that report'

'Little House on the Paul Daniels Magic Show': Well, it was there a minute ago

Whatever happened to decent British sitcoms? Ten suggested updates

Dad's UN Peace-Keeping Force
Steptoe and Son plc
It Ain't Half Hot without the Ozone Layer, Mum
The Unreconstructed Chauvinist Lads
Man about the Housing Trust
Till Divorce Us Do Part
Open All Hours on Sunday
Last of the Beaujolais Nouveau
Teri and June
On the Privatised Buses

TV times – the ten laws of television viewing

You invariably miss one part of a three-part serial

The remote control is always further away from you than the TV set

Commercial breaks aren't actually long enough for you to make a pot of tea

Programmes on TVs in shop windows seem more fascinating than the ones you get at home

The greatest excitement of the week is trying to guess the prices on *The Antiques Roadshow*

The greater the number of channels, the less there is that's worth watching

The film you hired from the video shop is always shown on TV the following week

If *The Match* ends up as 1–0, you always miss the moment when the goal is scored

Programmes you want to video are on at the same time

There's never anything worth watching on Tuesdays

Ten politically correct nursery rhymes

Height-Challenged Jack Horner

Little Ms Muffet

Mary, Mary, Quite Entitled to Exercise a Woman's Right to Change Her Mind

Differently-Abled Simon

This Intensively-Farmed Piggy went to Market

Three Visually Impaired Mice

Jack Spratt could Eat No Saturated Fat

Rap a Song of Six Pee

Pat-a-Cake, Pat-a-Cake Baking Operative

One, Two, Lace up a Trainer

The golden age of radio – ten cherished characters from *Round the Horne*

J Peasmold Gruntfuttock

Troilus Lackwind

Old Widow McGanderpoke

Dame Celia Molestrangler

Loombucket the Butler

Dr Gaylord Haemoglobin

Otto Von Kuckpowder

Revd Isambard Mousepractice

Beatrice Clissold

Spasm the Butler

Curtain Down I – ten short-lived theatrical productions

Beautiful People (1983) closed before the curtain went up on its first night at the Piccadilly Theatre

The Intimate Review (1950) closed during the interval of its first night at the Duchess Theatre

Thirteen for Dinner (1942) closed after one night at the Duke of York's Theatre

Casanova (1972), a musical, closed after one night at Liverpool's Empire Theatre

Frankenstein (1981) lasted one night on Broadway

Little Johnny Jones (1982), starring Donny Osmond, closed after one night on Broadway

Forty Love (1979) lasted three days at the Comedy Theatre

Top People (1984) lasted four days at the Ambassadors Theatre

The Merchant (1977) closed after four performances on Broadway

Carrie (1988) closed after five days on Broadway

Curtain down II – ten plays which were banned in Britain

Mrs Warren's Profession (George Bernard Shaw): banned in 1916 because the profession was prostitution

A View From the Bridge (Arthur Miller): banned in 1950 because it dealt with homosexuality

Six Characters in Search of an Author (Luigi Pirandello): banned in 1925 because it mentions incest

Early Morning (Edward Bond): banned in 1967 because it suggested a lesbian relationship between Queen Victoria and Florence Nightingale

Follow My Leader (Terence Rattigan): banned in 1938 because it dealt with Nazism

Children's Hour (Lillian Hellman): banned in 1951 because it dealt with lesbianism

A Patriot for Me (John Osborne): banned in 1964 because of its treatment of homosexuality

Tobacco Road (Jack Kirk): banned in 1937 because of the 'tough language and depravity of its characters'

The Last Mile (John Wexley): banned in 1930 as 'too tense for a London audience'

The Day that will End (Gordon Kennedy): banned in 1967 because of its treatment of the Kennedy assassination

No drones – Fry and Laurie as Jeeves and Bertie

What Ho! Ten partnerships of Jeeves and Wooster

Stephen Fry and Hugh Laurie (*Jeeves and Wooster*, ITV series, 1990)

David Suchet and Simon Cadell (*Right Ho, Jeeves*, Radio 4, 1988)

Michael Denison and John Quentin (Croft Original TV commercial, 1987)

Michael Hordern and Richard Briers (*What Ho, Jeeves*, Radio 4, 1980)

Edward Duke and Edward Duke (*Jeeves Takes Charge*, one-man stage show with Duke playing both characters, 1980)

Jack Watling and Derek Nimmo (*Carry On, Jeeves*, stage show, 1976)

Michael Aldridge and David Hemmings (*Jeeves*, Andrew Lloyd Webber musical, 1975)

Dennis Price and Ian Carmichael (*The World of Wooster*, BBC television series, 1965)

Deryck Guyler and Naunton Wayne (*Right Ho, Jeeves*, Radio 4, 1956)

Arthur Treacher and David Niven (*Thank You, Jeeves*, film, 1936)

Off the shelf – ten literary works which were banned

Black Beauty (Anna Sewell): banned in Namibia in the 1970s because of its title

Alice's Adventures in Wonderland (Lewis Carroll): banned in Hunan province, China, in 1931 for 'putting human beings and animals on one level'

Billy Bunter (Frank Richards): banned from Ipswich Public Library in 1970 as 'hurtful to fat boys'

Catcher in the Rye (J D Salinger): banned by the town of Boron, California, in 1989 for containing the word 'goddam'

Huckleberry Finn (Mark Twain): banned in Massachusetts in 1885 as 'trash suitable only for slums'

The Joy of Sex (Alex Comfort): banned in Ireland from 1974 to 1989

King Lear (William Shakespeare): banned in Britain in 1788 because of George III's madness; ban rescinded in 1820

Sherlock Holmes (Sir Arthur Conan Doyle): all Sherlock Holmes stories were banned in the USSR in 1929 because Conan Doyle dabbled in the occult

The Naked and the Dead (Norman Mailer): banned in Australia and Canada in 1949 as obscene

On the Origin of Species (Charles Darwin): banned in Tennessee in 1925 as irreligious and immoral

Man Bites Dog – ten genuinely newsworthy headlines

England Manager Must Stay

Ollie Warns: Watch Your Units!

Record Fall in Crime Figures

Britons Sweep Board at Wimbledon

Briton Reaches Second Round at Wimbledon

Minister Admits: 'I Don't Know'

Major Gives up Watching Test Matches to Run the Country

Liverpool: Jewel of the North

Sun Forecast for Bank Holiday

Charles and Diana: The Perfect Partnership

Changing sex! Ten men who wrote as women (and vice versa)

Sir Walter Scott (Chrystal Croftangry)
Charlotte Brontë (Currer Bell)
William Thackeray (Hon Wilhelmina Amelia
   Skeggs)
Mary Kingsley (Lucas Malet)
Harriet Beecher Stowe (Christopher Crowfield)
Mary Anne Evans (George Eliot)
Voltaire (Catherine Vadé)
Daniel Defoe (Penelope Firebrand)
Henry Adams (Frances Snow Crampton)
Aurore Lucie Dupin (George Sand)

File under 'Berserk' – ten authors' names from the British Library Catalogue

Arngrim Berserk   Wallop Brabazon
Mercedes Formica   O Heck
Florence A Baglehole   Ole Bagger
Manfred Lurker   Cornelius Crocus
Negley Teeters   Stuyvesant Fish

What *can* they make of it all? Ten British TV programmes sold abroad

Some Mothers Do 'Ave 'Em (Ethiopia)
Miss Marple (Indonesia)
Fawlty Towers (Nepal)
Coronation Street (Thailand)
You Rang, M'Lord? (Chad)
Are You Being Served? (Sri Lanka)
Tom Brown's School Days (Guatemala)
Dad's Army (Oman)
All Creatures Great and Small (Angola)
The Dick Emery Show (Abu Dhabi)

Ten video compilations we're waiting for

The Classic Gasps of Dan Maskell
Advertising Jingles: the Karaoke Tape
Sports Presenters' Hair: the Highlights
The Gold Blend Saga
The Best of Crimewatch
The Life of Brian: three Decades of Football
   Commentary
Collected Budget Speeches
The Rise and Fall of TV-am
The Clothes Show: 100 Sweaters from *A Question
   of Sport*
Party Political Broadcasts: the Thatcher Years

Ten sponsored Shakespeare plays

Do-It-All's Well That Ends Well
Much Asda About Nothing
Alfa Romeo and Juliet
Big Mac Beth
Fred Perrycles
Twelfth Night Nurse
The Merry Wives of Windsmoor
Timex of Athens
King Lear Jet
Hamlet

Unfunny export – trouble in store for Sri Lanka

Ten key dates in the development of the game show

940BC: King Solomon gives away a baby in the first ever quiz show

1025: King Canute proves it is impossible to hold back the tide of game shows which will flood Britain

1066: William the Conqueror wins the forerunner of *Bullseye*

1170: Henry II asks: 'Who will rid me of this turbulent priest?' All four contestants get the right answer

1192: Richard the Lionheart plays *Name that Tune* while imprisoned in Austria

1415: Henry V leads his team to a *Jeux Sans Frontières* win at Agincourt

1492: Columbus discovers the home of the game show

1509: Henry VIII proves an eager *Blind Date* contestant, but none of his six dates works out

1917: Russian revolution later finds its egalitarian ideals expressed in *Everybody's Equal*

1928: Birth of Bob Monkhouse

Paperback writers – the first ten Penguin books (1935)

Ariel (André Maurois)
A Farewell to Arms (Ernest Hemingway)
Poet's Pub (Eric Linklater)
Madame Claire (Susan Ertz)
The Unpleasantness at the Bellona Club (Dorothy L Sayers)
The Mysterious Affair at Styles (Agatha Christie)
Twenty-Five (Beverley Nichols)
William (E H Young)
Gone to Earth (Mary Webb)
Carnival (Compton Mackenzie)

Elementary! Ten new cases for Sherlock Holmes

The Strange Case of the Funny Little & Large Sketch
The Incredible Case of the Prompt Meter Reader
The Mystery of Richard Clayderman's Sales Figures
The Unusual Case of Drinkable English Wine
The Odd Case of the Soviet Leader's Sudden Illness
The Baffling Affair of the Nice Cup of Instant Tea
The Intriguing Case of the Cheerful Farmer
The Recurring Case of the Broken Cash Dispenser
The Missing Case of the Package Holidaymaker
The Unbelievable Case of the Jeans That Fitted

Ten memorably named Dickens' characters

Chevy Slyme (*Martin Chuzzlewit*)
Conkey Chickweed (*Oliver Twist*)
Tite Barnacle (*Little Dorrit*)
Nicodemus Boffin (*Our Mutual Friend*)
Quebec Bagnet (*Bleak House*)
Count Smorltork (*The Pickwick Papers*)
Sophy Wackles (*The Old Curiosity Shop*)
Morleena Kenwigs (*Nicholas Nickleby*)
Barnet Skettles (*Dombey and Son*)
Paul Sweedlepipe (*Martin Chuzzlewit*)

Bob, heir to greatness? A big question

Ten new magazines for the 1990s

Marxism Yesterday
Father and Baby
Non-Essentials
Goodbye!
Post-New Woman
Hansard Colour Supplement
Time In
House & Garden Repossession
Wimmin's Own
Country Death

Mr Bean – left
speechless

Ten of the easiest jobs in television

Wardrobe mistress on *Baywatch*
Script writer on *Whose Line Is It Anyway?*
Cameraman on *Points of View*
Make-up artist on *Rugby Special*
Props man on *Mastermind*
Director on *The Weather Forecast*
Dialogue coach on *Mr Bean*
Casting director on *The Sky At Night*
Stunt arranger on *Songs of Praise*
Actor on *Neighbours*

The first presenters of ten long-running TV programmes

A Question of Sport (1970): David Vine
Points of View (1961): Robert Robinson
Top of the Pops (1964): Jimmy Savile
Grandstand (1958): Peter Dimmock
Blue Peter (1958): Leila Williams and Christopher Trace
Panorama (1953): Patrick Murphy
Tomorrow's World (1965): Raymond Baxter
This Week (1956): Leslie Mitchell
Newsnight (1980): Peter Snow and Peter Hobday
Come Dancing (1950): Sylvia Peters

FOR THE RECORD

Who was Nosey Parker (and other news behind the names)?

Nosey Parker: Sixteenth-century Archbishop of Canterbury, Matthew Parker, who had a long nose and an inquisitive nature

Kilroy: James J Kilroy, an inspector in an American shipyard in the 1940s, who wrote 'Kilroy was here' on equipment to show it had been tested

Gordon Bennett: James Gordon Bennett II, owner of the *New York Herald* and the man who sent Stanley to Africa in search of Livingstone

Sweet Fanny Adams: Seven-year-old girl murdered in the early nineteenth century, whose dismembered body was found in a Hampshire river

Mickey Finn: Irish bartender in Chicago who drugged his customers before robbing them

Bloody Mary: Mary Tudor, who had over 300 'heretics' burnt at the stake during her short reign

The Real McCoy: World welterweight boxing champion Kid McCoy, who was billed as 'The Real McCoy' after conning an opponent into not training by pretending he was sick

Granny Smith: Maria Ann Smith, the first person to grow the tart green apples, in Australia in the 1860s

John Doe: Fictional name used in legal proceedings in the fourteenth century for witnesses who did not want their identity revealed

Silly Billy: King William IV, who had a penchant for rude jokes and an irresponsible attitude to his regal duties

Kids' stuff – ten children named after famous people

Woody Allen named his son, Satchel, after Louis 'Satchmo' Armstrong

Neneh Cherry named her daughter, Tyson, after Mike Tyson

Nicky Henson named his son, Keaton, after Buster Keaton

Paul Young named his daughter, Levi, after Levi Stubbs

Gyles Brandreth named his daughter, Aphra, after Aphra Behn

Bruce Willis and Demi Moore named their daughter, Rumer, after Rumer Godden

Ricky Schroder named his son, Holden, after William Holden

Dave Stewart and Siobhan Fahey named their son, Django, after Django Reinhardt

Mickey Stewart named his son, Alec, after Alec Bedser

Bryan Ferry named his son, Otis, after Otis Redding

Bright lights – the last ten towns to be granted city status

Sunderland (1992)	Cambridge (1951)
Derby (1977)	Lancaster (1937)
Bangor (1974)	Plymouth (1928)
Swansea (1969)	Salford (1926)
Southampton (1964)	Portsmouth (1926)

Selling abroad – ten people who have made ads overseas

Sting (*Kirin beer, Japan*)
David Bowie (*Sake, Japan*)
Robert Morley (*British Airways, USA*)
Boy George (*Shochu, Japan*)
Penelope Keith (*Heinz, Australia*)
Lloyd Cole (*Amaretto, Italy*)
Ringo Starr (*Renown, Japan*)
Felicity Kendal (*Flora, Australia*)
Jeffrey Archer (*Suntory, Japan*)
Sean Connery (*Ito Ham, Japan*)

Felicity butters it up . . .

. . . as Sting puts it down

The origin of ten household names

Lego: from the Danish 'leg godt', meaning 'play well'

Hovis: from the Latin 'hominis vis', meaning 'man's strength'

Durex: an abbreviation from durability, reliability, excellence

Bovril: from the Latin 'bo', meaning ox, and 'vril' from 'vrily', a name given to the life force in an obscure nineteenth-century novel

Castrol: because it was originally made from castor oil

Nivea: from the Greek word meaning 'snow white'

Quink: an abbreviation of 'quick drying ink'

Harpic: from the first three letters of the first name and surname of the man who developed it, Harry Pickup

Findus: from the words 'fruit industries'

Vim: from the Latin meaning 'with strength'

Ten Essex men

Dudley Moore (Dagenham)
Michael Nicholson (Romford)
Mike Smith (Hornchurch)
Rik Mayall (Harlow)
John Fowles (Leigh-on-Sea)
Ian Holm (Ilford)
Bobby Moore (Barking)
Neil Innes (Danbury)
Sir Alf Ramsey (Dagenham)
Michael Wilding (Westcliff-on-Sea)

Ten Essex girls

Charlotte Rampling (Sturmer)
Sandie Shaw (Dagenham)
Jilly Cooper (Hornchurch)
Juliet Stevenson (Kelvedon)
Millicent Martin (Romford)
Joan Sims (Laindon)
Sarah Miles (Ingatestone)
Maggie Smith (Ilford)
Alison Moyet (Basildon)
Jenny Powell (Ilford)

Ten people who are known by their middle names

Henry Warren Beatty
Ruz Fidel Castro
Alfred Alistair Cooke
Isaac Vivian Richards
Vivian Clive James
Ruth Bette Davis
Ernestine Jane Russell
Leonard James Callaghan
Christopher Rob Andrew
Norvell Oliver Hardy

Essex? It's posher playing polo – Jilly

Charlotte – from Sturmer to silver screen

Purely academic – a league table of exam results

Richard Branson (no O-levels)
Peter de Savary (one)
Betty Boo (two)
Steve Wright (three)
Gary Lineker (four)
Paul Daniels (five)
Phillip Schofield (six)
Annie Lennox (seven)
Amanda de Cadenet (eight)
Prince Edward (nine)
Anneka Rice (ten)

From beyond the grave . . . ten odd legacies

In 1974 dentist Philip Grundy left dental nurse Amelia White £181,000 on condition that she didn't go out with men or wear any make-up or jewellery for five years

In 1960 Samuel Bratt, whose wife would not let him smoke, left her £330,000 on condition that she smoked five cigars a day

The Rev John Gwyon, who killed himself in 1929, left nearly £10,000 in trust to buy knickers for local boys

In 1856 German poet Heinrich Heine left his estate to his wife on condition that she remarry so 'there will be at least one man to regret my death'

In 1990 an unnamed benefactress left £100,000 to King Edward VII's Hospital for Officers for the 'expansion, improvement and maintenance of its lavatories'

In 1977 Ernest Digweed left £26,000 to Jesus provided the public trustees could obtain proof 'which shall satisfy them of His identity'

In 1765 John Hart left his brother George a gun and a bullet 'in the hope that he will put the same through his head when the money is spent'

Buenos Aires businessman Juan Potomachi left £30,000 to the Teatro Dramatico in 1955 provided his skull was used in *Hamlet*

David Davis left Mary Davis five shillings in 1788 'to enable her to get drunk for the last time at my expense'

In 1987 teacher Hensley Nankivell stipulated that any relative wishing to benefit from a legacy of £400,000 must first train as an airline pilot

It's all in the stars, Yasmin – Amanda

GLUCK!

CLOBBLE! CLOBBLE!

WORLD'S FIRST CHURKEY

Goodbye, Columbus – ten of this year's less celebrated anniversaries

135 years ago toilet paper was first manufactured

35 years ago the world's first musical potty was patented

200 years ago Philip Le Brocq patented the portable mangle

55 years ago the first churkey, a cross between a chicken and a turkey, was bred

100 years ago the first fairground big wheel, the brainchild of George Washington Ferris, was erected in Chicago

50 years ago the mayor of New York banned pinball machines

150 years ago the first operation using anaesthetic was performed

200 years ago John Ashley patented a design for a flushing lavatory

600 years ago Jacques Gringonneur designed the playing card pack we know today, with clubs, hearts, diamonds and spades

75 years ago Major Leone Sextus Denys Oswolf Fraudati Tollemache-Tollemache de Orellana Plantaganet Tollemache Tollemache died in the First World War trenches

Ten couples who were born on the same day

Pauline Collins and Raquel Welch (September 3, 1940)

Anthony Andrews and Brendan Foster (January 12, 1948)

Robert Palmer and Dennis Taylor (January 19, 1949)

Peter Gabriel and Stevie Wonder (May 13, 1950)

Geoff Boycott and Manfred Mann (October 21, 1940)

John Motson and Virginia Wade (July 10, 1945)

Harvey Smith and Jon Voight (December 29, 1938)

Michael Grade and Lynn Redgrave (March 8, 1943)

Penelope Keith and Marvin Gaye (April 2, 1939)

Francis Coppola and David Frost (April 7, 1939)

Ten couples who died on the same day

Orville Wright and Mahatma Gandhi (January 30, 1948)

Maria Callas and Marc Bolan (September 16, 1977)

Josef Stalin and Sergei Prokofiev (March 5, 1953)

Orson Welles and Yul Brynner (October 10, 1985)

Sammy Davis Jr and Jim Henson (May 16, 1990)

Sir Malcolm Sargent and Woody Guthrie (October 3, 1967)

Joyce Grenfell and Zeppo Marx (November 30, 1979)

Otto Preminger and Jim Laker (April 23, 1986)

David Niven and Raymond Massey (July 29, 1983)

Clark Gable and Gilbert Harding (November 16, 1960)

Now it can be told! The names behind the initials

G K Chesterton (Gilbert Keith)

J M Barrie (James Matthew)

P J O'Rourke (Patrick Jake)

W C Fields (William Claude)

J P R Williams (John Peter Rhys)

F R Leavis (Frank Raymond)

P D James (Phyllis Dorothy)

J R R Tolkien (John Ronald Reuel)

H L Mencken (Henry Louis)

A J P Taylor (Allan John Percivale)

Soap stars – ten people who have advertised those handy household products

Alan Freeman (Omo)
Liza Goddard (Lenor)
Jimmy Young (Flash)
Simon Le Bon (Persil)
Frank Windsor (Tide)
Christine Truman (Daz)
Tony Blackburn (Fairy Liquid)
Val Doonican (Dreft)
Jill Gascoigne (Flash)
Craig Douglas (Fairy Snow)

Just fancy that! The origin of ten phrases

'Drink a toast': Pieces of toast used to be dropped into wine to collect sediment

'Eat humble pie': Umbles were the less savoury parts of a deer, given to the lower orders after a hunt

'To go berserk': After a demented Norse warrior, Berserker, who wore only a bearskin in battle

'A toady': A charlatan's assistant who pretended to swallow poisonous toads, to be miraculously 'cured' by the doctor's bogus medicines

'Honeymoon': From the German tradition of drinking honey wine for a month after a wedding

'Let the cat out of the bag': An eighteenth-century fraud where a cat was substituted for a suckling pig and sold in a sack at county fairs

'Apple pie bed': From the French *nappe pliée*, meaning folded sheet

'At sixes and sevens': Two London livery companies argued for 150 years about which should be sixth and seventh in order of precedence

'White elephant': Siamese courtiers could be ruined by the cost of keeping an albino elephant, a gift from a malicious king

'Sell someone down the river': Rebellious American slaves were sold to cruel plantation owners at the lower end of the Mississippi

New! Improved! Simon is the housewives' choice

Forever young – the ages of ten cartoon characters

Rupert Bear (72)
Desperate Dan (55)
Dick Tracy (61)
Superman (54)
Wonder Woman (50)
Dennis the Menace (41)
Batman (53)
Snoopy (42)
Spiderman (30)
Jane (60)

You know the series – but can you name the hospital?

Casualty (Holby City Hospital)
St Elsewhere (St Elgius)
Doctor Kildare (Blair General)
Angels (St Angela's)
Doogie Howser MD (Eastman Medical Centre)
Ben Casey (County General)
The Young Doctors (Albert Memorial)
Doctor in the House (St Swithin's)
Emergency (Rampart Hospital)
Medics (Henry Park Hospital)

Life goes on – ten people born on the day a famous person died

Johnny Rotten and A A Milne (January 31, 1956)
Frank Zappa and F Scott Fitzgerald (December 21, 1940)
Adam Ant and Henri Matisse (November 3, 1954)
Richard Stilgoe and Sergei Rachmaninov (March 28, 1943)
Jimmy Savile and Harry Houdini (October 31, 1926)
Telly Savalas and Lenin (January 21, 1924)
Donna Summer and Sir Malcolm Campbell (December 31, 1948)
Che Guevara and Emmeline Pankhurst (June 14, 1928)
Anthea Redfern and Ernest Bevin (April 14, 1951)
Billie Jean King and Lorenz Hart (November 22, 1943)

Linda – plenty of roll, but hold the rock

Well-hung – ten people who have had their paintings exhibited

Tony Curtis	Bryan Ferry
Joni Mitchell	Ronnie Wood
Desmond Morris	Sylvester Stallone
Prince Charles	Miles Davis
Anthony Quinn	Adolf Hitler

Name brands – ten people who launched their own products

Burt Reynolds (jewellery)
Joan Collins (jeans)
Paula Yates (underwear)
Fran Cotton (sportswear)
Linda McCartney (vegetarian frozen food)
Shakira Caine (jewellery)
Ken Kercheval (popcorn)
Paul Newman (salad dressing)
Princess Stephanie (swimwear)
Pepsi & Shirlie (girls' clothes)

Ten people born on Boxing Day

Henry Miller	Irene Handl
Mao Tse-Tung	Richard Widmark
Denis Quilley	Rohan Kanhai
Jane Lapotaire	Richard Skinner
Thomas Gray	Phil Spector

Return ticket – ten people who appeared more than once on *Desert Island Discs*

Arthur Askey (four times)
Peter Ustinov (three)
Robertson Hare (three)
Stanley Holloway (three)
Celia Johnson (three)
Eva Turner (three)
Emlyn Williams (three)
Earl Hines (three)
Roy Plomley (two)
Tommy Steele (two)

One thousand years of history – ten people who made it to 100

Manny Shinwell (Labour politician)
Irving Berlin (songwriter)
Catherine Bramwell-Booth (Commissioner of the Salvation Army)
Gwen Ffrangcon-Davies (actress)
Grandma Moses (American painter)
Naruhiko Higashikuni (Japanese prime minister)
Sir Robert Mayer (founder of children's concerts)
Adolf Zukor (chairman of Paramount Pictures)
Rose Kennedy (matriarch of the Kennedy clan)
Moses (well-known list-maker)

Child's play – a top ten of motherhood

Lulu (one child)
Wendy Craig (two)
Joan Collins (three)
Linda McCartney (four)
June Brown (five)
Loretta Lynn (six)
Alice Thomas Ellis (seven)
Soraya Khashoggi (eight)
Rose Kennedy (nine)
Victoria Gillick (ten)

The name game – ten people named after other people (or things)

Sebastian Coe: Sebastian from Shakespeare's *The Tempest*
Dustin Hoffman: Dustin Farnum, silent screen star of the 1920s
Glenn Hoddle: Glenn Miller
Sugar Ray Leonard: Ray Charles
Rumer Willis, daughter of Bruce: Rumer Godden, novelist
(Michael) Colin Cowdrey: The MCC
Bing Crosby: Bingo, a character in *The Bingsville Bugle*
Shirley 'Big Daddy' Crabtree: Charlotte Brontë's novel *Shirley*
Everton Weekes: Everton Football Club
Doris Day: Doris Kenyon, silent film star

Doris, winner of the name game

Ahead of their time – ten achievements of youth

Youngest person to have an entry in *Who's Who*: Yehudi Menuhin at the age of fifteen

Youngest to win an Oscar: Shirley Temple in 1934, aged six

Youngest MP: Edmund Waller, who took his seat in 1623 at the age of sixteen

Youngest Brain of Britain: Anthony Carr, sixteen, in 1956

Youngest golfer to hole in one: Coby Orr from Texas in 1975, aged five

Youngest British chess grand master: Michael Adams, in 1989, aged seventeen

Youngest artist elected to the Royal Academy: Sir Thomas Lawrence at the age of twenty-three

Youngest player to appear in a first-class competitive soccer match: Eamonn Collins, for Blackpool in 1980, at the age of fourteen

Youngest university student in Britain: Ganesh Sittampalam, who started at Surrey University in 1990 at the age of eleven

Youngest millionaire: Jackie Coogan, child star who made $1m when he starred in *The Kid* with Charlie Chaplin in 1920, aged five

Life before soap – ten soap stars' former jobs

William Roache (Ken Barlow, *Coronation Street*): army captain

Johnny Briggs (Mike Baldwin, *Coronation Street*): opera singer

Ken Kercheval (Cliff Barnes, *Dallas*): sold plots in a cemetery

Pam St Clement (Pat Butcher, *Eastenders*): journalist

Ian Smith (Harold Bishop, *Neighbours*): scriptwriter for *Prisoner: Cell Block H*

Norman Bowler (Frank Tate, *Emmerdale*): deckboy on oil tanker

Elizabeth Dawn (Vera Duckworth, *Coronation Street*): assistant in Woolworth's

Brian Regan (Terry Sullivan, *Brookside*): apprentice with Liverpool FC

Lynn Perrie (Ivy Brennan, *Coronation Street*): cabaret singer

Bill Treacher (Arthur Fowler, *Eastenders*): ship's steward

The shampoo set – ten people who worked in hairdressers' shops

Danny De Vito
Twiggy
Lewis Collins
Greta Garbo
Divine
Limahl
Charlie Chaplin
Alison Moyet
Yves Montand
Perry Como

Sweet charity – ten Unicef ambassadors

Roger Moore
Julio Iglesias
Harry Belafonte
Sir Edmund Hillary
Imran Khan
Youssou N'Dour
Audrey Hepburn
Sir Richard Attenborough
Liv Ullmann
Sir Peter Ustinov

Pam, well versed in dead-lines

Anneka, a girl guy for tonight

It makes you proud to be British – ten organisations which are

British Academy of Experts
British Council of Shopping Centres
British Army Wrestling Association
British Origami Society
British Association of Former United Nations Civil Servants
British Compressed Air Society
British Christmas Tree Growers' Association
British Automatic Sprinkler Association
British Essential Oils Association
British National Committee for Electro-Heat

The day thick waists were banned (and other strange offences)

Women with waists measuring more than thirteen inches were barred from the court of Catherine de Medici

Books on geography and astrology were banned in England in the 1550s because they were feared infected with magic

The cultivation of potatoes was outlawed in France in the 1630s because they were suspected of causing leprosy

In sixteenth-century England, husbands were banned by law from beating their wives after 10 pm

Turks caught drinking coffee in the sixteenth century risked being executed

People in eighteenth-century central America risked excommunication if they imbibed drinking chocolate

Residents of Minnesota were banned from hanging out underwear of different sexes on the same washing line

Elizabeth I of Russia banned everyone apart from herself from wearing pink, and those flouting her rule could be punished by mutilation

Philip the Fair of France forbade single women from owning more than one dress

Pigs were once banned from the streets of France after one caused an accident involving a member of the royal family

The girls in blue – ten former girl guides

Glenda Jackson
Mandy Rice-Davies
Kim Wilde
Judith Chalmers
Anneka Rice

Sinitta
Helen Sharman
Virginia Bottomley
Gloria Hunniford
Anna Massey

I'm free! Ten people awarded freedom of the City of London

Angela Rippon
Michael Gambon
Cliff Richard
Terry Venables
Rodney Bewes

Derek Nimmo
Prunella Scales
Clare Francis
Jan Leeming
Martyn Lewis

Down to earth – ten people who have jumped with the Red Devils

Jim Davidson
Tom Baker
Ian Ogilvy
Louis Collins
Tony Blackburn

Sarah Kennedy
Matthew Kelly
Phillip Schofield
Suzanne Dando
Kathy Tayler

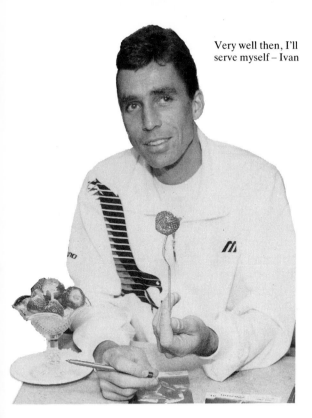

Very well then, I'll serve myself – Ivan

The Stormin' Norman factor – ten other men who have received honorary knighthoods

Ronald Reagan (1989)
Sidney Poitier (1974)
François Mitterrand (1984)
Alistair Cooke (1973)
Caspar Weinberger (1988)
Douglas Fairbanks Jr (1949)
Paul Mellon (1974)
Bob Geldof (1986)
Lech Walesa (1991)
King Hussein of Jordan (1984)

Straight down the middle – ten amateur golfers who have holed in one

Graham Gooch   Danny Kaye
Henry Cooper   Bob Hope
Richard Nixon   Cliff Michelmore
Freddie Garrity   Brian Jacks
Mike Reid   Jimmy Tarbuck

Ten only children

John Mortimer   Leslie Crowther
Annie Lennox   Robert De Niro
Clark Gable   Elton John
Ivan Lendl   John Lennon
Frank Sinatra   Alexander Solzhenitsyn

Thicker than water – ten celebrity cousins

Ginger Rogers and Rita Hayworth
Jon Snow and Peter Snow
Cyrille Regis and John Regis
Rip Torn and Sissy Spacek
Jerry Lee Lewis and Jimmy Swaggart
Clive Allen and Paul Allen
Brian Wilson and Mike Love
Natasha Richardson and Jemma Redgrave
Clive Lloyd and Lance Gibbs
The Queen and Lord Lichfield

Jimmy's a one-shot wonder – geddit?

Congratulations, it's a book! Ten people who have given birth to baby books

Julie Walters (*Baby Talk*)
Nigel Planer (*Good Enough Dad*)
Jane Asher (*Keep Your Baby Safe*)
Peter Mayle (*Baby Taming*)
Libby Purves (*How Not To Be A Perfect Mother*)
Paula Yates (*The Fun Don't Stop*)
Bill Cosby (*Fatherhood*)
Patricia Hewitt (*Your Second Baby*)
Esther Rantzen (*Baby Love*)
Penny Junor (*Babyware*)

Lucky for some – ten people born on Friday the thirteenth

Samuel Beckett (April 1906)
Christopher Plummer (December 1929)
Peter Davison (April 1951)
Zoe Wanamaker (May 1949)
Clive Barnes (May 1927)
Jane Glover (May 1949)
Michael Spinks (July 1956)
Howard Keel (April 1917)
Peter Scudamore (June 1958)
Graham 'Suggs' McPherson (January 1961)

University challenge – ten subjects studied by celebrities at college

Rowan Atkinson (electrical engineering)
Paul Simon (English)
William Roache (medicine)
Jonathan Ross (East European modern history)
Harry Enfield (politics)
Anna Ford (economics)
John Cleese (law)
Chrissie Hynde (art)
David Gower (law)
Chris Lowe (architecture)

Time for a change, Nigel – Ben

History? Moi? Jonathan gets a lesson from David Cassidy

Six pounds in a week? It's a disaster!

Write on – what graphology reveals about your job

Full of intricate loops: *You're a highway planning officer*

Shaky: *Inner-city schoolteacher*

Almost illegible: *Student doctor*

Lots of crossings out: *Channel ferry captain*

Well spaced out: *Member of an acid house band*

Surrounded by blobs: *Sumo wrestling coach*

Long sweeping strokes: *Street cleaner*

Sloping to the right: *Member of the Cabinet*

Sloping to the left: Guardian *leader writer*

Heavily underlined: *Carpet fitter*

Divided by a common language – a guide to the differences between English and American

Gas: *Americans get gas from a petrol station; Britons gets gas from real ale*

Trunks: *In the United States, trunks hold the spare tyres of cars; in Britain they hold the spare tyres of men on the beach*

Fall: *Americans have falls after the long days of summer; Britons have falls after long nights in the pub*

Turkey: *In America, a turkey is a disaster; in Britain, a turkey is a disaster that happens on Christmas Day*

Rubbers: *Americans wear rubbers to go fishing; Britons wear rubbers when they don't want to catch anything*

Fags: *In America, there is a powerful lobby in favour of fags; in Britain there is a powerful lobby against them*

Suspenders: *In America, they keeps men's trousers up; in Britain they make men want to take their trousers down*

Drugstore: *In America, drugstores are on street corners; in Britain they're in teenagers' pockets*

Football: *An American game where the players are in mortal danger; a British game where the spectators are in mortal danger*

Bill: *In America, bills fill your wallet; in Britain they empty it*

Dreams – a guide to interpretation

You dream of drowning: *You're going on a camping holiday in Scotland*

Flying: *You're stuck in the departure lounge at Gatwick*

Suffocating: *You're planning a trip to the first day of the January sales*

Being buried alive: *You're asleep on a commuter train in the rush hour*

Being burned alive: *You forgot to turn off the electric blanket*

Being involved in a terrible disaster: *You've got tickets for a Jive Bunny concert*

Being chased by a hideous monster: *Mortgage rates are going up again*

Devouring a giant Big Mac: *You've eaten the duvet*

Endlessly falling: *The cat's asleep at the top of the stairs*

Walking naked in the street: *You've had too much to drink and you're not dreaming*

Ten food additives they don't warn you about

The one in bread rolls that makes people at rugby club dinners want to throw them

The one in lobster that makes your bank balance turn red

The one in spaghetti that gives it a mind of its own

The one in taramasalata that makes you want to smash plates

The one in beer that makes you think you're Frank Sinatra

The one in spinach that makes it stick to your teeth

The one in peanuts that makes it impossible to leave any in the bowl

The one in cream crackers that makes them break when you butter them

The one in sausages that sets the grill on fire

The one in baked beans

The world's ten oldest punchlines

No, she went of her own accord

The breaststroke, sir

Arrows, officer? I didn't even see the bloody Indians

Yeth, and I'm only thixteen

You hum it and I'll play it

Why, are you coming apart?

Be quiet, sir, or they'll all want one

There's nothing queer about Carruthers

No, it's just the way I walk

To get to the other side

Will it be a hard winter? Ten signs to look for

TV weathermen fly south for the duration

The guards at Buckingham Palace are issued with moon boots

Both of London's gritting lorries go in for a service

The Pools Panel is put on permanent contract

Postmen are given sleigh-driving lessons

The polar bears at London Zoo go into hibernation

Brighton puts in a bid for the Winter Olympics

Nobody camps outside Harrod's for the first day of its January sale

The central heating boiler blows up

British Rail blame 'penguins on the line'

BR regrets . . .

Don't string me along, Parker – Lady Penelope

Ten shattered childhood illusions

The cast of *Thunderbirds* are really puppets
The cast of *Neighbours* aren't
The tooth fairy doesn't use your old teeth for
  anything
Treets do melt in your hand
The Milky Bar Kid is a forty-seven-year-old
  midget
The presenters of *Blue Peter* read from a script
Eating crusts doesn't make your hair curl
The pop charts are based on returns from one shop
  in Goole
The contestants on *Blind Date* are all unemployed
  actors
Avoiding the cracks in pavements doesn't mean
  you won't have bad luck

Has arts sponsorship gone too far? Ten tell-tale productions

The King and ICI
Natwest Side Story
My Fair Lada
Me and My Chelsea Girl
Puss in Boots the Chemist
Guys and Dolcis
A Tale of Two MFI Settees
Some Like it Hotpoint
The Merry Scottish Widow
Eau What a Lovely War

Ten more entries from the alternative dictionary

Absentee: *A missing golf accessory*
Awestruck: *Hit with a paddle*
Getting uptight: *Waking up drunk*
Gigolo: *A love-homing man*
Oyster: *A Cockney crane driver*
Parachutist: *Person who jumps to contusions*
Shock absorber: *BBC duty officer*
Spanish Armada: *A series of Juan-liners*
Toady: *A man who stoops to concur*
Wife: *A woman whose divorce hasn't quite worked
  out*

The Gold Blend saga continues – ten new plot developments

They fall out when she catches him with another woman – a tea lady

They have a huge row over who washes up the coffee cups

They both lose their jobs because all that caffeine makes them too tired for work

She recoils from kissing him because of his 'coffee breath'

They finally go to bed together as a threesome – him, her and a Thermos flask of Gold Blend

They get married and receive fifteen espresso machines as presents

Their teeth turn the colour of mahogany

He sustains a hernia while carrying all their old coffee jars to the local bottle bank

They set up Coffee Drinkers Anonymous

They have a baby and call him Maxwell House

Don't you know there's a recession on? Ten Second World War slogans worth recycling

They also serve who save their waste

Few books bear second reading – comb your bookcase for salvage

Equip the Forces with your rubber oddments

Remember, it is an offence to write a letter on one side of the paper only

Keep your toothpaste tubes to help make torpedo tubes

If of waste you don't take heed, you ignore your country's need

Put it in the bank, it'll help to buy a tank

Don't forget to give all your used bones to salvage

To win this scrap you must save scrap

Make room by your fireside for the lonely stranger

The ten most pointless things in the world

Gazing out of the window on a Tube train

Saying 'Come on, come on' to a red traffic light

Urging your horse on while watching the Grand National on television

Writing 'I hope I've got your address right' in a letter

Looking at the stereo when listening to a CD

Saying 'And this is the bathroom' when showing prospective buyers around your house

Changing queues at the post office

Sending a stamped addressed envelope to America

Gesticulating while on the telephone

Returning the 'No' envelope expecting to win the prize draw

Do you have a weight problem? Ten tell-tale signs

The lift buzzes when you get in – even when you're alone

The water in your bath amounts to no more than three pints

You consider sumo wrestling an art form

Your private health insurance company suggests a group rate

Your tailor uses a theodolite instead of a tape measure

You dream of being as thin as Roseanne

The local boy scouts use your old raincoat as a marquee

You are at the complete mercy of shoe salesmen

You need an HGV licence to drive a car

Your local Weightwatchers goes ex-directory

Is it all too much? Ten forms of occupational madness

Supermarket managers go off their trolleys
Train drivers go loco
Greeks lose their marbles
Stunt pilots go loopy
Dustmen flip their lids
Call girls go bonkers
Heavy metal fans go off their rockers
Greengrocers go bananas
Cricketers go batty
Plumbers go round the bend

The bald facts – ten positive things about having no hair

You look no more ridiculous than usual in a
   swimming cap
You'll never go grey
Instead of 'wash and go' you can just go
You can tell precisely where to stop shaving
Someone might mistake you for Sean Connery
It's the perfect cure for dandruff
No more 'Are you going on holiday this year?'
   conversations with hairdressers
You don't look quite such a mess first thing in the
   morning
No more tortured decisions to make when
   hairstyles change
No more hairs in the sink

Ten alternatives to sell-by dates

Perfume: *Smell-by date*
Aspirins: *Get-well-by date*
Superglue: *Seal-by date*
Portable phones: *Give us a bell-by date*
Shoes: *Sole-by date*
Throat lozenges: *Yell-by date*
Hair cream: *Gel-by date*
Long-life batteries: *Duracell-by date*
Prawns: *Shell-by date*
Story cassettes: *Tell-by date*

Are you insecure? Ten tell-tale signs

You think the actors are looking at you when you
   go to the theatre
You have shoulder pads in your pyjama jacket
When someone addresses you as 'Sir' you look
   behind you
You joined an assertiveness training course under
   a false name
You never go to restaurants in case you can't
   understand the menu
You apologise to the speaking clock for calling late
   at night
Your carpet slippers have lifts on them
You've filled two pages of your passport with
   'distinguishing marks'
You always think the photofits on *Crimewatch*
   look like you
Your 25-yard swimming certificate is framed and
   hangs above the mantelpiece

Made for each other – ten places which should be twinned

Clint (North Yorkshire): Eastwood
   (Nottinghamshire)
Shirley (Derbyshire): Temple (Cornwall)
Whitney (Hereford & Worcester): Houston
   (Strathclyde)
Dean (Devon): Martin (Lincolnshire)
Gordon (Borders): Banks (Cumbria)
Kirk (Highlands): Douglas (Isle of Man)
Stirling (Central): Moss (South Yorkshire)
Charlton (Wiltshire): Heston (Greater London)
Winston (Durham): Churchill (Avon)
Dudley (West Midlands): Moore (Cheshire)

Inscrutable or what? Ten Chinese proverbs

Only a fool attempts a somersault in an oyster shell
An egg should never argue with a stone
Even a broken drum can save the moon
A half-empty teapot is a noisy affair
If a west wind blows at the summer solstice, prepare to catch shrimp in the gutter of your roof
A generation of men is like a white colt jumping over a crevasse
Never talk pygmy to a dwarf
Good luck comes like a large watermelon sitting in the middle of a freshly-tidied room
Bean curd lifted on a sliver of bamboo is bound to hang down
Every elbow bends inwards

Getting the wind up – the Beaufort Scale explained

Force 1: Smoke from the barbecue follows you round the garden
Force 2: Money-off coupon forms drift around your front door
Force 3: British Rail discovers a new excuse
Force 4: Everyone south of Watford adopts the Dunkirk spirit
Force 5: The barbecue follows you round the garden
Force 6: Terry Wogan advised to stay indoors
Force 7: John Prescott demands a public inquiry
Force 8: Ben Johnson breaks the world 100-metres record
Force 9: Bernard Manning anchored to the ground
Force 10: Slates blown back on to prison roofs

Ten of the world's greatest rarities

A cathedral without scaffolding
A National Express coach in the slow lane
French school parties queueing
A retirement party for a football manager
A shopping precinct without a market researcher
A British tennis player with a can of silver polish
A worn-out police boot
A carpet warehouse without a sale
A politician accepting the blame
A happy ending in *Brookside*

Ten more entries from the alternative dictionary

Carouse: *Liverpudlian garage*
Cellulite: *To give short measure*
Delegate: *Entrance to the capital of India*
Distaff: *The Princess of Wales's entourage*
Endorse: *The last nag past the winning post*
Khaki: *Used to start the car*
Likelihood: *Juvenile delinquent*
Monsoon: *Male Scot on the eve of his eighteenth birthday*
Porpoise: *Bad deportment*
Retail: *Miracle of veterinary surgery*

Terry, having a gale of a time

This noisy Britain – ten places to give you sleepless nights

Thundersley (Essex)
Loudwater (Buckinghamshire)
Bangor (Gwynedd)
Rattlesden (Suffolk)
Great Snoring (Norfolk)
Splatt (Cornwall)
Clatter (Powys)
Nether Wallop (Hampshire)
Coughton (Warwickshire)
Belchford (Lincolnshire)

Outlook predictable – ten sure-fire weather indicators

Drought minister appointed: anyone know how to build an ark?
Friday night: two days of rain ahead
Monday morning: cloudless sky
Christmas Day: no snow
Bonfire night: showers towards evening
Bank Holiday: worst weather since records began
Wimbledon: torrential downpour
Michael Fish is smiling: second consecutive day of sunshine
Michael Fish isn't smiling: British summer starts here
You go abroad: glorious sunshine all over Britain

Ten artists for the National Gallery's Sainsbury Wing

Salvador Deli
Claude Monet-Off
Francis Bacon
Leonardo da Vimto
Henri Mattissons

Beryl Cook-Chill
Joseph Turnover
Andy Warholsten-Pils
Pablo Picashew
Eugene Delacroissant

Signing off – ten appropriate ways to end a letter

'Yours unfaithfully' (Relate)
'We remain' (Any funeral director)
'Yours gratefully' (British Coal)
'Best regards' (Moorfields Eye Hospital)
'Up yours sincerely' (Bob Geldof)
'Lots of love' (Lawn Tennis Association)
'Your faithful servant' (Any mother)
'Yours ever – and ever and ever' (Spiritualist Association of Great Britain)
'Yours all ways' (Cynthia Payne)
'Yours cordially' (Alcoholics Anonymous)

Sir Bob, sincerely got up

OK Judge, hand over that wig real easy now – final court of appeal

After the Birmingham Six . . . ten cases the Court of Appeal has yet to hear

The Renault 5
The G7
The After 8
The Winchester 73
The Britvic 55
The Famous 5
The Magnificent 7
The Indianapolis 500
The Fun Boy 3
The Pennsylvania 65000

Time to go home – ten signs that the party's over

The hostess begins to hum the national anthem
You find yourself talking to the milkman
Someone gets out Trivial Pursuit
The only thing left to drink is a bright green
　liqueur
You've sobered up
You've woken up
Someone puts on a Leonard Cohen tape
You happily stub out your cigarette in a vol-au-
　vent
Shortly afterwards, you eat the vol-au-vent
You go into the garden to look at the stars

Are your acting days over? Ten tell-tale signs

Your last theatre job was understudy to the
　usherette
You're asked to do the warm-up at state funerals
You specialise in one-man shows – one man shows
　up to watch
You sell your life story to the local freesheet
Your agent goes ex-directory
People mistake you for Michael Fish
You decide to enter politics
The *Sun* couldn't care less about your private life
You move from opening supermarkets to
　shoplifting from them
You play 'third villain' in *Crimewatch*
　reconstructions

It makes you think – ten mysteries of life

Why is there always a grey glove under the back seat of the bus?

Where did the man who invented patents register his idea?

Why do sex surveys always make you feel inadequate?

Why are ants always in such a hurry?

Why can't you watch a medical programme without being convinced you've got the illness under discussion?

Why are men's ages in direct proportion to the number of socks they get at Christmas?

Are incompetent proof reader unobservnat?

Why do people say it's an impossible question when they mean it's an impossible answer?

What do plainclothes policemen wear when they're off-duty?

Why does flammable mean the same as inflammable?

I had a terrible dream last night . . .

I was trapped in a lift with Lionel Blair – in his tap shoes

My son was exposed as the child who beaned Prince William

Liverpool was chosen as European City of Culture

The new colour for autumn was John Major grey

Loyd Grossman came to dinner

All money was the same size as the 5p piece

I was picked for the Welsh Rugby Union team

I stood in for Jeremy Beadle

I picked up the phone and Brian Hayes was on the other end

My story was read out on the Simon Bates sob slot

And then I pressed Ground Floor – Lionel

On the sick list – a guide to interpretation

'It must have been something I ate': *It must have been something I drank*

'I think I'm going down with something': *Down to the links with my golf clubs*

'I've got a temperature': *Hasn't everybody?*

'I've got terrible back trouble': *Every time I think of work I don't want to go back*

'I've got an appointment with the doctor': *He's my squash partner*

'I'm worried I might have strained something': *My boss's credulity*

'I've got some sort of bug': *Isn't English wonderfully vague?*

'I just feel really hot all the time': *It's a glorious day and I'm sunbathing*

'I've got that three-day flu that's going round': *I'm not going to miss this opportunity*

'I picked something up in the office': *And we're off to the coast for the day*

Ten signs of a misspent youth

A beer belly at 21

Fruit-machine elbow

A Hawkwind T-shirt

A one-volume library (dog-eared paperback of *Lady Chatterley's Lover*)

A 'Get Well' card from Ladbrokes

Perfect recall of the theme songs to *The Hillbillies, Mister Ed* and *Gilligan's Island*

Over 200 car windscreen sunstrips with different girls' names on them

Several court orders for child support

Taking less than ten minutes to finish on a double at darts

One O-level (in biology)

Completely barking – ten new dog breeds

German pointer: Freezes at the first sight of a sunbed with a towel on it

St Bernardweiler: Drinks its own barrel of brandy and runs amok during the après-ski

Highland springer: Scottish breed partial to designer mineral water

Wire-haired Old English sheepdog: Not only does the painting, but rubs the woodwork down first

Prince Charles spaniel: Floppy-eared dog, often to be found barking at plants

Afghan retriever: Useful for police work at hippy festivals

Baby setter: Good with children, but can clear out the contents of a fridge within an evening

Toy alsatian: In case Action Man ever turns to crime

Pit bull beagle: Smokes forty a day of its own accord

Miniature chihuahua: Small enough to be a Christmas-cracker novelty

Ten more entries from the alternative dictionary

Jury: *The only thing which doesn't work properly when it's fixed*

Televangelist: *A man who is ecumenical with the truth*

Barbecue: *A line of men waiting for a haircut*

Library: *A multi-storey building*

Baked bean: *A wind instrument*

Industrial spy: *A mugger of invention*

Surrogate motherhood: *Cash-on-delivery*

Olympic mile: *An extinct race*

Poltergeists: *See-through nickers*

Critic: *Someone who gives the job the best jeers of his life*

Cor Blimey – Dick's a Herbert

Ten oriental philosophies popular with teenagers

Noh Kandu: Trance-like state induced by the prospect of tidying the bedroom

Ree Bok: Ability to find large amounts of cash for fancy trainers

Yo: The art of communication without using recognisable speech

Soh Wot: Intellectual detachment from the affairs of the world

Intendo: Putting off to tomorrow what could be done today

Def Too: Withdrawal from the world through use of a personal stereo

See Yoo: Martial art popular in Scotland

Li Lo: Staying in bed until lunchtime

Noh Way: Mystical response to any parental request

Chuk Tikka: Terrible penance induced by too much lager and an Indian meal

Ten alternative fairground attractions

The water chute: *Players' tunnel at Wimbledon*

Ghost train: *Any British Rail station on a Sunday morning*

Dodgem cars: *Hyde Park Corner*

Candyfloss stall: *Mills & Boon section at W H Smith*

Fortune-teller: *Open your bank statement*

Punch and Judy show: *House of Commons during Prime Minister's question time*

Haunted House: *House of Commons during the rest of the week*

Test your strength: *Sit through a whole episode of Young Doctors*

Rollercoaster ride: *Invest in the stock market*

Whiplash: *Take a ride on a hopper bus*

Don't remind me! Ten things which haunt the famous

David Bowie: *The Laughing Gnome*

Glenda Jackson: Doing TV commercials for Hanson Trust

Lord Dacre: Authenticating the Hitler Diaries

Pete Townshend: Writing 'Hope I die before I get old'

Yusuf Islam: Cat Stevens

Warren Beatty: *Ishtar*

Neil Kinnock: *That* rally

Dick Van Dyke: His Cockney accent in *Mary Poppins*

James Callaghan: 'Crisis? What crisis?'

Prince Charles: Plants

Ten words which are everywhere, but no one actually uses

Dwelling	Gratuities
Beverage	Patrons
Affix	Purchases
Garment	Receptacle
Alight	Remittance

Ten things which can only be a matter of time

A 'Save the Pit Bull Terrier' campaign
Banks charging for admission
Crisp-flavoured crisps
A Paul Gascoigne junior surgeon's kit
A Royal Family shares flotation
Boil-in-the-bag water
A convincing John Major impression
A European Commission ban on fish and chips
A Darling Buds of May fashion range
A one-man army (British)

Ten phrases that tempt fate

It's all over bar the shouting
Leave it to me, I've got the magic touch
I never burn, I tan
I don't foresee any problems
I've been driving for twenty years and have never had an accident
I have a natural affinity with things mechanical
Surely England can't lose now
I've never failed yet
I've never even met our doctor
I'd be surprised if it was anything serious

Ten local heroes

Billy Preston	Michael York
Johnny Bristol	Rod Hull
Melissa Manchester	Belinda Carlisle
Burt Lancaster	Angelo Dundee
Mick Fleetwood	Charlie Chester

But how much tea is there in China? The real meaning of ten clichés

'Blood is thicker than water': *If the relative density of water is indexed as 1.00, blood is slightly thicker at 1.06*

'A hairsbreadth': *The average hair is 1/48" in diameter*

'A king's ransom': *The largest recorded regal ransom was 150,000 marks paid to the Holy Roman Emperor, Henry VI, for Richard the Lionheart*

'Only skin-deep': *The deepest human skin is found on the back, where it can grow up to 1/5" thick*

'In the wink of an eye': *An average wink takes one-tenth of a second*

'Time immemorial': *A thirteenth-century English law decreed that time immemorial began with the reign of Richard I in 1189*

'Just a moment': *An old English time unit defines a moment as 1½ minutes*

'Peppercorn rent': *In the 1640s, Dutch East India Company traders were allowed into Japan if they paid rent with much-prized peppercorns*

'As old as the hills': *The oldest rock on earth dates back 3096 billion years*

'All the tea in China': *Recent figures put China's tea production at just over half a million tonnes a year*

Michael – York's favourite swashbuckler

Just think! Ten things to keep you awake at night

What if David Icke is right?

Someone may have put your name forward for *Surprise Surprise*

Our next monarch's closest confidante could be a geranium

As a member of Mensa, Jimmy Savile is one of the most intelligent people in Britain

How do they know the Thames Barrier will work?

What if Kylie Minogue has another three sisters at home?

Cliff Richard could be only halfway through his showbusiness career

Somebody still has the negatives from last year's office party

It's taken two million years of evolution to produce Little & Large

Jeremy Beadle might be lurking when you try to light a barbecue

Three sisters? The cheek of it! – Kylie

Ten replacements for a pit bull terrier

A poodle with a grudge
A bonsai sumo wrestler
John Prescott with a muzzle
Hannibal Lecter
An East End pub landlady
Someone who's just been wheel-clamped
A Leeds United supporter
Roseanne Barr
A VAT inspector
A South African policeman

Ten handy excuses for not cutting the grass

There's so much junk in the garden shed I can't find the mower

I was thinking of getting a goat

I'm trying to cultivate a wildflower meadow

I'm waiting for the grass to choke the weeds

There's a European Community regulation against it

It provides perfect cover for sunbathing

I'm trying to persuade David Attenborough to use it for his next series

I wouldn't want to give the moles a headache

It needs a good raking first

There's so much junk in the garden shed I can't find the rake

Hello, hello – ten French towns which don't sound it

Relevant	Rang
Dôle	Consolation
Hem	Apt
Parent	Job
Ramble	Fixin

Making a spectacle of yourself – ten signs that you need glasses

You hail fire engines at bus stops
You have to assume the lotus position to read the bathroom scales
You steam up the screen when watching television
You get a black nose reading the newspaper
Everything comes into focus when you're drunk
You frequently apologise to lamp-posts
At the theatre you ask for seats in the orchestra pit
You can't get close enough to your toenails to cut them
You compliment hatstands on what they're wearing
You're the only one at the cinema with opera glasses

All doshed up – Loadsamoney

Inside story – the real contents of the chancellor's budget box

A copy of *The Bluffer's Guide to Economics*
His dinner money
A clean change of underwear
A lucky Zürich gnome
Four litres of Scotch and 5000 cigarettes
A wax effigy of the previous chancellor and a hatpin
A list of Bernard Manning's six best replies to hecklers
A copy of his parents' wedding certificate
A ready-reckoner from a Christmas cracker
A one-way air ticket to Paraguay

The woof guide – what your dog says about you

Poodle: *Former member of Mrs Thatcher's cabinet*
Beagle: *You're a heavy smoker*
Afghan hound: *Your specialist subject on Mastermind is the sixties*
Old English sheepdog: *You're a DIY fanatic*
Bloodhound: *You work for the Inland Revenue*
Guide dog: *You design sweaters for contestants on A Question of Sport*
Mongrel: *You support proportional representation*
Whippet: *Oxfam sends you doggy bags*
Corgi: *One has one's regal pretensions*
Greyhound: *You can't get to the pub quick enough*

Are you a bore? Ten tell-tale signs

You empty the kitchen at parties
Jehovah's Witnesses make their excuses and leave
Answerphones hang up on you
You're still doing Loadsamoney impressions
You go misty-eyed talking about the sixties
Your record collection is in alphabetical order
You're still complaining about decimalisation
Whoever you're talking to is eager to introduce you to someone else
Your bedroom is a shrine to Elvis
You eat steak and chips in foreign restaurants

It makes you think – ten more mysteries of life

Why is it always easier to get out of bed when you don't have to?
Where does Tarzan get such a good haircut?
Why don't people who snore wake themselves up?
Why do theatregoers put on their best clothes to sit in the dark for three hours?
Where can you get a poetic iicence?
If vampires can't see their reflections in mirrors, how does Count Dracula shave?
Why don't authors bring out cover versions of other people's novels?
How come nobody ever phones TV chefs just when they're putting the peas on?
Why is there only one word for thesaurus?
Why do you never get pestered by single-glazing salesmen?

Fangs ain't what they used to be – ten unknown members of the Dracula family

Vlad the Inhaler: Suffers from chronic catarrh

Vlad the Derailleur: Travels round on a mountain bike

Vlad the Retailer: Bleeds his customers white

Vlad the Descaler: Specialises in the removal of plaque from fangs

Vlad the Impala: Assumes the form of a blood-crazed antelope

Vlad the Shaw Taylor: Happy to help the police with their inquiries

Vlad the Akela: Organiser of the dreaded Transylvanian cub-scouts

Vlad the Wholesaler: All your vampire needs catered for

Vlad the Loudhailer: Social embarrassment in restaurants

Vlad the Hotelier: Dracula weekends a speciality

Gary – Rococo Loco

Ten more entries from the alternative dictionary

Draughtsman: *Someone who always works to rule*

Shot-putter: *The power behind the thrown*

Lavatory cistern: *The power behind the throne*

Optician: *A cornea shop*

Teacher: *Someone who gets paid to come to terms with children*

Female auditor: *A lady of ledger*

Prostitute: *A woman whose business is definitely picking up*

Phrenologist: *Someone who likes to press a head*

Traffic jam: *A toot ensemble*

Three-furlong marker: *A gallop pole*

A holidaymakers' guide to B&Bs

The strip light above the sink mirror never works

You discover that pink candlewick bedspreads still exist

There is a burn mark inside the lampshade of the bedside light

However long the flex, you can't manoeuvre your hairdryer anywhere near a mirror

The veneered wardrobe was made in the 1950s and is big enough to house the costumes of a West End musical

But there are only three wire coathangers

By the time you get to use it, the shared bathroom looks as if it's been used for a talcum powder fight

You would never get up so early for breakfast if you were at home

It's impossible to have a normal conversation at breakfast, but embarrassing to sit there saying nothing

You try to work out how much the owners are making each night

Know your angst from your ergo – a plain man's guide

'Auteur': *Person whose name appears on screen before everyone else's*

'Angst': *Posh nerves*

'Ergo': *Stands to reason, dunnit?*

'Rococo': *Gary Glitter's stage costumes*

'Eclectic': *Plagiarism they can't sue over*

'Zeitgeist': *What's hot and what's not*

'Recherché': *Not for the likes of you and me*

'Schadenfreude': *I'm all right, Jack*

'Weltanschauung': *Point of view*

'Existential': *You've only got yourself to blame*

Ten new products based on the Swiss Army knife

Italian army knife: Has an ice-cream scoop
Dutch army knife: Has an implement for getting stones out of clogs
French army knife: Has a garlic crusher
Irish army knife: Has a potato peeler
Japanese army knife: Has a mini ritual sword
Chinese army knife: Has a spare bicycle spoke
Greek army knife: Has a kebab skewer
American army knife: Has a switchblade
British army knife: Has been cut to one blade only
Korean army knife: Has a dog whistle

The brain drain – ten computer viruses to watch out for

Shakespeare: *Company accounts turned into verse form*
Joyce: *All punctuation removed*
Picasso: *The 'I's appear at a funny angle*
Dante: *Files spontaneously combust*
Lawrence: *All words reduced to four letters*
Plato: *Obeys commands, but now wants to know why*
Stockhausen: *Makes meaningless noises at you*
Hockney: *Produces endless, highly-priced print-outs*
Freud: *Cuts access to memory to one-hour-a-week session*
Madonna: *Screen turns blue*

What's bugging David?

Ten predictions by Nostradamus re-interpreted

'The exiles shall spread internal strife': *Rolling Stones to tour Britain*
'Cities will be vexed by sudden change': *One-way systems*
'The bird of prey shall offer himself to the earth': *Eddie Edwards to make a comeback*
'A great mass of men will arise from the land of the Slavs': *Boris Yeltsin blows it*
'All Europe will be much astonished and bleeding': *British soccer clubs allowed back into international competition*
'The great pretender shall be brought down': *Gazza's knee goes in another tackle*
'The land and sea of Italy shall be bloody': *Package holidays to the Adriatic*
'The writings of the prophet shall fall into the hands of the tyrant': *Labour's spending plans leaked to the* Sun
'There will be wailing and moaning and it shall not cease': *Commuting on Network South-East*
'The great queen shall be beset by vipers': *Mrs Thatcher can't say she wasn't warned*

How's business? Ten ways to go bankrupt

Plumbers: Go down the plughole
Painters and decorators: Go to the wall
Car dealers: Crash
Toilet paper manufacturers: Go down the pan
Deep-sea divers: Go under
Dieticians: Go belly up
Bra manufacturers: Go bust
Travel agents: Pack up
Drug companies: Go down the tubes
Glaziers: Go broke

Don't just do something, sit there! Ten of the world's dullest jobs

Set designer for *News At Ten*
Lyricist for a Hare Krishna album
Copywriter for government health warnings
Navigator on the Isle of Wight ferry
Chief taster at a mineral water plant
Groundsman at an astroturfed stadium
Scriptwriter for the speaking clock
Editor of the telephone directory
Cardboard-city planner
Prompter for a mime artist

Snap happy – ten things you'll find when you get your holiday film developed

A labrador wearing sunglasses and a headscarf
Granny putting her knickers on under a towel
Someone 'holding up' the Leaning Tower of Pisa
A leather-faced fisherman mending his nets
Someone pouring sangria over his face from a
    long-spouted jug
An ancient ruin you don't remember visiting
A collapsed sandcastle with its architect in tears
A flash-photo of a group of red-eyed people in a
    taverna
The couple you promised to keep in touch with
A green smudge on a khaki background (actually a
    lizard on a dirt road)

Danger – Chat Show Host At Work

Health risks – ten occupational diseases

Channel tunnel workers: Gaulstones
Carpet fitters: Piles
Sheep farmers: Diptheria
Airline pilots: Flu
Scottish goalkeepers: Dropsy
Carpenters: Cold saws
Chat-show hosts: Parkinson's disease
Beachcombers: Shingles
Politicians: Foot-in-mouth disease
Painters: Distemper